GRILLING MAESTROS

Volume 3

GRILLING MAESTROS

Volume 3

Produced by Marjorie Poore Productions
Photographs by Alec Fatalevich

Sponsored by

CONTENTS

Introduction 6

Soups, Starters, and Light Meals

Grilled Chilled Gulf Shrimp with Cucumbers, Tomatoes, and Peanut Oil Dressing 11

Potato, Leek, and Watercress Soup with Grilled Smoked Duck 13

Grilled Tomato and Fennel Soup with Grilled Soft-Shell Crabs 15

Cedar-Planked Brie with Roasted Garlic and Peppers 17

Grilled Mediterranean Garden Sandwich 18

Portobello Mushroom and Goat Cheese Sandwich 21

Eggplant Stacks with Roasted Corn Vinaigrette 22

Caponata Bruschetta 24

Grape Leaf–Wrapped Camembert with Bacon and Roasted Onion Topping 26

Shrimp Parfait with Lucifer Cocktail Sauce 27

Aluminum Foil Potatoes with Sexy Sauces 31

Margarita Wings 32

Poultry

Grilled Boneless Breast of Chicken with Grapes, Parsnips, and Toasted Almond Basmati Rice 37

Grilled Marinated Chicken with Cauliflower, Celery, Red Onion, and Quinoa Salad and Herbed Yogurt Dressing 39

Grilled Turkey Meat Loaf with Hand-Cut Fries 41

Turkey Drumsticks Slathered with Barbecue Sauce and Potato Hash 43

Devil's Brewed Roast Chicken with White Trash BBQ Sauce and Grilled Vegetable Salad 45

Grilled Chicken and Vegetable Fried Rice 46

Grilled Thanksgiving BBQ Turkey Casserole 48

Meat

Grilled Pork Loin Medallions with Apples, Turnips, and Caramelized Onion Grits 53

Grilled Lamb Loin with Onions, Potatoes, Cabbage, and Herbs 55

Grilled Veal Chop with Root Vegetables and Rosemary Cream 56

Grilled Szechuan-Style Skirt Steak with White Mushrooms, Spinach, and Black Pepper Dressing 58

Grilled Pork Tenderloin with Shrimp, Broccoli, Country Ham, and Toasted Peanut Butter 59

Grilled Bison Fillet with Arugula, Garbanzo Beans, and Spicy Peanut Sauce 60

Grilled Sausage, Portobello Mushrooms, and Vegetables with Marinated French Lentils 63

Grilled Saddle of Lamb with Coconut Pears 65

Tagliate with Arugula and Grilled Vegetables 67

Bodacious T-Bone Steaks with Sexy Barbecue Sauce 68

Grilled Pork Steak with Warm Potato Salad 69

Grilled Angus Steak with Assorted Grilled Peppers, Grilled Garlic, and Gorgonzola 70

Decadent Steak Oscar 72
Better Butter Burger 73
Grill Wok Flank Steak Fajitas 75
Apple Ginger Pork Chops with Grilled Apple
    Rings and Corn Bread 77
Grilled Veal Chops with Mushroom Fricassee
    and Buffalo Mozzarella 78
Pulled Pork Sundaes 80
Thick-Cut Bone-In Southwest Pork Chop with
    Chipotle and Corn Stuffing 83
Stuffed Pork Baby Back Ribs with Curried
    Fruit Compote 84

Seafood

Grilled Mahi Mahi and Sautéed Backfin
    Crabmeat with Zucchini, Spinach, and
    Cream 89
Grilled Shrimp with Avocado Sweet Corn
    Relish 90
Grilled Sea Scallops with Black-Eyed Peas,
    Cabbage, Tomatoes, and Slab Bacon 91
Grilled Salmon with Chilled Pink Grapefruit,
    Spicy Black Beans, and Rice 93
Grilled Salmon with Lavender Butter and
    Grilled Mangos 95
Grilled Mackerel with Black and Green Beans,
    Tomatoes, and Anchovy Pesto 96
Bacon-Wrapped Trout with Rosemary and
    Warm Smashed Potatoes Debbie-Style 98
Grilled Monkfish with a Pan Roast of Oysters,
    Wild Mushrooms, Spinach, and Leeks 100

Grilled Catfish Fillet and Asparagus with
    Potatoes, Carrots, and Turnips 102
Grilled Tuna and Vegetable Bagna 104
Trout with Fennel, Dill, and Potatoes 105
Grilled Rainbow Trout with a Warm Salad of
    Grilled Sweet Potatoes, Grapes, Belgian
    Endive, and Pumpkin Seeds 106
Grilled Sea Bass in Aluminum Foil 108
Poached Sea Bass and Vegetables in Green
    Peppercorn Cream 109
Texas Surf and Turf: Jumbo Shrimp Wrapped
    in Beef Tenderloin 110
Banana Leaf–Wrapped Grouper with Jerk
    Butter and Honey Lemon Sauce 113
Grilled Halibut with Cucumber Horseradish
    Salad and Shrimp and Avocado Butter
    Sauce 114
Cedar-Planked Salmon Pinwheels 116
Prosciutto-Wrapped Salmon and Scallops with
    Maple Chili Glaze and Red Beet Salad 117
Cedar-Planked Sea Bass with Roasted Red
    Pepper, Crab, and Bacon Crust 118

Acknowledgments 121

Index 122

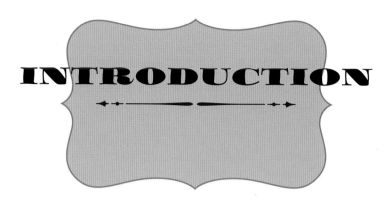

INTRODUCTION

Welcome to the world of the "grilling maestros"! This is our third collection of recipes from the three master grillers, Marcel Desaulniers, Ted Reader, and Fritz Sonnenschmidt, who can be seen every week on the national public television series *Grilling Maestros.* Once again, they have put together an irresistible collection of delicious, fun, and easy-to-prepare recipes, suitable for all grillers, from beginners to advanced.

The popularity of grilling has grown dramatically in the last fifteen years as more and more people discover the fun and excitement of cooking outdoors. It is a terrific way to get together with family and friends, to enjoy the open air and escape a stuffy kitchen on hot summer days. In response to this increasing popularity, the market now offers an amazing array of grills, tools, and other accoutrements that can instantly earn you a grilling "black belt." Augment your skills with items such as flavored woods and chips, impeccably designed charcoal and gas grills ranging from highly portable miniatures to monster-sized grills that can easily handle the

requirements of the hungriest block party, and extensive choices of rubs, marinades, and sauces that add layers of flavor and punch to your food.

Grilling Maestros Volume 3 is here to provide you with the last part of the equation: wonderful recipes that can take you into new grilling dimensions. Glance through this book and see that nearly everything you can make in your kitchen can be adapted for outdoor cooking. But even with these tempting recipes in hand, be aware that there are some essential techniques that are critical to successful grilling. The biggest challenges seem to occur in the following areas: cooking food to the "correct doneness," and understanding the difference between *direct heat and indirect heat* cooking methods.

Cooking food to correct doneness: A meat thermometer — something that even professionals rely on — can be one of your best friends at the grill. Cooking food to the *correct doneness* is a matter of taste, but is also an important safety concern. Study internal temperature guides, and remember that even after food has been taken off the grill, the internal temperature will continue to rise for several minutes, and food will continue to cook. If you're grilling vegetables, get to know which ones require longer cooking, and need to be parboiled or precooked before being placed over direct heat.

Indirect versus direct heat cooking methods: With *direct heat* cooking, the heat source or fire is directly under the food. It is used for quick-cooking items such as steaks, chicken breasts, hamburgers, and vegetables needing less than 25 minutes of cooking time. Usually, the longer something takes to cook, the less direct heat exposure it requires. *Indirect heat* is similar to oven roasting and is used for items that require longer cooking time, such as roasts, whole chickens, and ribs. The heat source is not directly under the food, but next to it, so the heat can rise, bounce off the grill lid, and circulate all around the food.

(Remember that for both direct and indirect methods, it's critical to keep your grill lid on while cooking.)

There are other important grilling techniques that will help you earn and keep that grilling "black belt." We suggest you visit www.weber.com, which offers free instruction and information on a wide range of grilling-related topics. But the most important thing is to *practice!* The more you grill, the more skilled and confident you will become as you learn from your mistakes, develop a feel for the grill, and start trusting your own instincts and intuition.

And while you're practicing, we hope you'll try many of the mouthwatering recipes you find in this book, created by the *Grilling Maestros* — from their grills to yours!

SOUPS, STARTERS & LIGHT MEALS

Chapter 1

GRILLED CHILLED GULF SHRIMP
WITH CUCUMBERS, TOMATOES, AND PEANUT OIL DRESSING

Marcel Desaulniers

It is hard to resist this refreshing appetizer, which can be easily adjusted to make dinner-sized portions. To ensure perfectly succulent shrimp, remember to keep the skewers over low heat. – **Serves 4**

1 pound extra-large (16-20) Gulf shrimp, peeled and deveined

2 tablespoons olive oil

Salt and freshly ground black pepper

$3/4$ cup peanut oil

$1/4$ cup cider vinegar

1 teaspoon soy sauce

1 teaspoon Dijon mustard

1 teaspoon chopped fresh herbs

4 cucumbers (about 2 pounds), peeled, split in half lengthwise, seeds removed, and cut into long thin strips lengthwise

1 small head red leaf lettuce (about $1/2$ pound), cored, separated into leaves, washed, and dried

2 tomatoes (about $3/4$ pound), peeled, seeds removed, and chopped into $3/8$-inch pieces

$1/4$ cup dry-roasted peanuts (for garnish)

Lightly coat the shrimp with the olive oil. Season the shrimp with salt and pepper and thread them onto 4 skewers. Grill the shrimp over low heat for about 2 minutes on each side. Transfer the shrimp from the grill to the refrigerator on a large dinner plate and allow to cool enough to handle, about 10 minutes. Remove the shrimp from the skewers. With a paring knife, slice the shrimp in half lengthwise. Cover the shrimp with plastic wrap and refrigerate until needed.

In a medium bowl, whisk together the peanut oil, cider vinegar, soy sauce, mustard, and fresh herbs. Season with salt and pepper. Cover with plastic wrap and set aside at room temperature until needed.

To assemble, divide the cucumber strips evenly around the borders of 4 chilled plates, leaving a small well in the center. Arrange the lettuce leaves in the center of the plate in the cucumber well. Season the chopped and seeded tomatoes with salt and pepper. Divide the seasoned tomatoes evenly among the 4 plates in the center of the lettuce leaves. Arrange the chilled shrimp around each plate. Dress each of the chilled appetizers with about 3 tablespoons of the peanut oil dressing. Sprinkle the plates with the dry roasted peanuts. Serve immediately.

POTATO, LEEK, AND WATERCRESS SOUP
WITH GRILLED SMOKED DUCK

Marcel Desaulniers

The added step of brining in this recipe not only keeps the duck breasts especially moist, but also maximizes the absorption of flavors during the smoking process.
– Serves 4 to 6

½ cup kosher salt

2 tablespoons sugar

2 (10- to 12-ounce) duck breasts

1 ½ pounds leeks

2 tablespoons unsalted butter

1 onion, peeled and chopped

2 stalks celery, trimmed and chopped

1 clove garlic, peeled and crushed

Salt and freshly ground black pepper

6 cups hot chicken stock

1 ½ pounds potatoes, peeled, cut into 1-inch cubes, and covered with cold water

¼ cup half-and-half

1 large bunch watercress, trimmed, washed, and dried

Prepare a brine in a 3-quart nonreactive bowl by combining 1 cup warm water, the kosher salt, and sugar. Whisk to dissolve the sugar. Add 1 cup cool water and stir to combine. Set aside.

Trim all fat and membrane from the duck breasts. Place the duck breasts one at a time, in between two sheets of lightly oiled aluminum foil or parchment paper. Uniformly flatten each breast with a meat cleaver or the bottom of a heavy sauté pan. Immerse the duck breasts in the brine for 2 minutes, turning the breasts after 1 minute. Remove the breasts from the brine and pat dry with paper towels.

Line the top wire shelf of a smoker with parchment paper. Place the breasts on the shelf in the smoker and smoke for 2 hours at 225 degrees F. Remove the breasts from the smoker and grill them over low heat for 2 ½ to 3 minutes on each side. Remove the breasts from

the grill and cool at room temperature, then refrigerate, uncovered, until needed.

Remove the green tops from the leeks, discarding the tops or saving them for flavoring a stock. Cut the leeks in half lengthwise, and then rinse each half under cold running water while rubbing to remove grit or dirt. Cut the leeks into ½-inch-long pieces.

Heat the butter and 1 tablespoon water in a 5-quart saucepan over medium heat. When hot, add the leek pieces, onion, celery, and garlic. Season with salt and pepper, and cook for 5 minutes. Add the hot chicken stock.

Drain and rinse the potatoes under cold running water, and then add the potatoes to the saucepan. Bring the stock to a boil, and then reduce the heat and simmer slowly for 45 minutes until the potatoes are thoroughly cooked.

Remove the soup from the heat. Purée in a food processor fitted with a metal blade. Return the soup to the saucepan and heat to a low simmer. In a small saucepan or microwave oven, heat the half-and-half; when hot, add to the soup and stir gently to incorporate. Season with salt and pepper.

Cut the smoked duck breasts into thin strips. Heat the duck strips in a nonstick sauté pan over medium heat; when hot, remove from the heat.

Arrange equal portions of the watercress in a ring along the outside edge of each warm soup plate. Pour equal portions of the soup into each soup plate and sprinkle equal amounts of smoked duck strips over the soup. Serve immediately.

GRILLED TOMATO AND FENNEL SOUP
WITH GRILLED SOFT-SHELL CRABS

Marcel Desaulniers

"Soft-shell" refers to the molting stage at which a crab casts off its shell for a larger one. The entire crab is edible when harvested at this point and its sweet flavor is incomparable. When it's paired with a tangy tomato and fennel soup, the flavors are unforgettable. – **Serves 6**

2 tablespoons freshly squeezed lemon juice

2 tablespoons olive oil

Salt and freshly ground black pepper to taste

6 live jumbo soft-shell crabs, dressed

1 tablespoon vegetable oil

1 large onion, diced

1 tablespoon cider vinegar

1 tablespoon curry powder

12 tomatoes, washed, cored, cut in half, and grilled

6 cups chicken stock

1 tablespoon chopped fresh thyme

1 tablespoon cracked black peppercorns

2 small bay leaves

$\frac{1}{2}$ cup (1 stick) unsalted butter

1 $\frac{1}{4}$ cups all-purpose flour

1 large fennel bulb (about 1 pound), washed, cored, cut in half, grilled, and cut into thin strips

In a 3-quart nonreactive bowl, whisk together the lemon juice and olive oil. Season with salt and pepper. Whisk to combine. Add the dressed soft-shell crabs, and turn each a few times to coat with the marinade. Wrap each crab individually in plastic wrap, and refrigerate until ready to grill.

Heat the vegetable oil and 1 tablespoon water in a 5-quart saucepan over medium heat. When hot, add the onion. Season with salt and pepper and sauté 5 minutes. Add the cider vinegar and curry powder and whisk vigorously. Remove the saucepan from the heat. Cut the tomato halves into quarters and add them to the saucepan. Add the chicken stock. Tie the thyme, peppercorns, and bay leaves in a small piece of cheesecloth and add to the tomatoes. Return the pan to medium heat. Bring to a boil, lower the heat, and simmer for 25 minutes.

Melt the butter in a 3-quart saucepan over low heat. Add the flour and stir to make a roux. Stir and cook for 6 to 8 minutes, being careful not to scorch the roux. When the roux is cooked, strain 2 cups of the simmering stock into it. Whisk vigorously until smooth, and then add this mixture to the large saucepan with stock and tomatoes. Whisk until smooth. Simmer for another 10 minutes.

Remove the soup from the heat. Remove the cheesecloth bundle and discard. Purée the soup in a food processor fitted with a metal blade. Strain and return the soup to medium heat to simmer.

Heat the grilled fennel strips in a non-stick sauté pan over medium heat. Keep hot while grilling the crabs.

Beginning with the top soft-shell side first, grill the crabs over medium-high heat for about 1$\frac{1}{2}$ minutes on each side.

Ladle the soup into 6 warm soup plates. Place the hot fennel strips in the center of the soup in each plate and then top with a crab. Serve immediately.

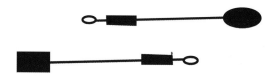

CEDAR-PLANKED BRIE WITH ROASTED GARLIC AND PEPPERS

Ted Reader

(Reprinted from The Sticks and Stones Cookbook, Macmillan Canada, 1999)

Make this treat for your next dinner gathering and get ready for accolades. Although baked Brie may be familiar, the method of planking is unusual, and a whole planked cheese makes quite the spectacular appetizer. The combination of melted cheese and a garlicky topping smeared onto great bread is terrifically good. You can easily make the topping the day before and refrigerate it until needed; let it warm to room temperature before adding the cheese. – **Serves 8 to 10**

2 small (¼-pound) wheels Brie

½ cup plus 2 tablespoons olive oil

2 heads garlic, separated and peeled

2 scallions, finely chopped

1 red bell pepper, roasted, peeled, seeded, and finely chopped

2 tablespoons chopped fresh thyme

2 tablespoons balsamic vinegar

2 teaspoons coarsely ground black pepper

Salt to taste

1 cedar plank, soaked in water for at least 12 hours before cooking

Preheat the grill to high heat.

With a sharp knife, scrape the rind of the top of each wheel of Brie to expose cheese. Set aside.

Heat ½ cup olive oil in a small sauté pan over medium-high heat and add whole cloves of garlic. Reduce heat to medium and simmer garlic in oil until softened and beginning to color, about 20 minutes. Remove from the heat, and using slotted spoon, transfer garlic to a small bowl to cool. Reserve the garlic-flavored oil for another use. Mash garlic cloves using the back of a fork. Add the scallions, red pepper, thyme,

balsamic vinegar, the remaining 2 tablespoons olive oil, and black pepper. Season with salt. Spread garlic and pepper mixture over the tops of the Brie wheels.

Place soaked plank on the grill, close the lid, and grill for 10 minutes or until it begins to crackle and smoke. Being careful of the smoke, open the lid and place cheeses on the plank. Close the lid and grill for 10 to 12 minutes until the cheese begins to melt and bubble. Remove the planked cheese from the grill. Serve with slices of crusty bread, flat bread, or crudités.

GRILLED MEDITERRANEAN GARDEN SANDWICH

Marcel Desaulniers

This healthful recipe is brimming with fresh flavors. The medley of grilled vegetables gets a tangy boost when topped with a Mediterranean olive mixture. Be sure to use a good quality olive, as the common canned variety will lack the intense flavor that bestows the Mediterranean flair. – **Serves 4**

2 large tomatoes

1 onion, thinly sliced

16 Mediterranean black olives, pitted and sliced

1/2 teaspoon chopped fresh thyme

1/4 teaspoon minced garlic

1 teaspoon plus 1/4 cup olive oil

1/4 teaspoon cider vinegar

1/4 teaspoon Dijon mustard

1/4 teaspoon freshly squeezed lemon juice

Salt and freshly ground black pepper to taste

8 slices country-style wheat bread

8 slices mozzarella, about 1/8 inch thick

1 zucchini, lightly peeled, sliced on an angle, 1/8 inch thick

16 spinach leaves, stemmed, washed, and dried

1/4 cup grated Parmesan cheese

Peel, seed and chop 1 tomato. Combine the onion, chopped tomato, olives, thyme, and garlic in a noncorrosive bowl. In a separate bowl, whisk together 1 teaspoon of the olive oil, cider vinegar, Dijon mustard, and lemon juice. Combine the olive oil mixture with the onion mixture, and season with salt and pepper. Cover with plastic wrap and refrigerate for 1 hour.

Brush both sides of each bread slice lightly with the remaining 1/4 cup olive oil. Arrange 4 slices of bread on a clean, dry work surface. Place a slice of mozzarella on each piece of bread. Equally divide the zucchini in an even layer over the mozzarella on each slice of bread. Season the zucchini lightly with salt and pepper. Slice the remaining tomato into eight 1/8-inch-thick slices. Place 2 tomato slices on top of each

zucchini layer, and again season lightly with salt and pepper. Drain any excess liquid from the onion mixture and equally divide on top of the tomato slices. Top each portion with another slice of mozzarella and a slice of bread to form the sandwich.

Grill the sandwiches over low heat for 2 minutes on each side. Place the sandwiches on a nonstick baking sheet, place the baking sheet on the grill, and close the cover. Heat for about 5 minutes, until just hot throughout. Remove the sandwiches from the grill and separate each sandwich into two halves, placing 4 spinach leaves and sprinkling 1 tablespoon Parmesan cheese in the center of each. Rejoin the halves and cut each sandwich in half. Serve immediately.

PORTOBELLO MUSHROOM AND GOAT CHEESE SANDWICH

Fritz Sonnenschmidt

(Reprinted from Weber's Big Book of Grilling, Chronicle Books, 2001)

Portobello mushrooms are a cousin of the commonly cultivated white mushroom. Their strong, earthy taste and dense texture make them an extremely popular alternative to meat. The stems tend to be woody and are often removed in recipes such as this. Reserve the stems for marinades, stocks, or soups—they can be frozen for up to 6 months. – **Serves 4**

4 fresh portobello mushrooms (about 5 ounces each)

2 red or yellow bell peppers (6 to 8 ounces each)

2 yellow squashes (about 6 ounces each), ends trimmed

1 large ripe tomato (about 8 ounces)

1/2 cup olive oil

1 tablespoon chopped fresh rosemary

1 tablespoon finely chopped shallot

1/2 teaspoon kosher salt plus extra to taste

1/4 teaspoon freshly ground black pepper plus extra to taste

3 tablespoons balsamic vinegar

8 (1/2-inch-thick) slices soft-crusted French or Italian bread, or soft rolls

8 ounces fresh goat cheese

12 to 16 fresh basil leaves

Remove the stems from the mushrooms. Cut the bell peppers in half lengthwise. Remove the seeds and flatten the peppers with the palm of your hand. Cut the squashes lengthwise into 1/2-inch-thick slices. Cut the tomato crosswise into 1/2-inch-thick slices. Place the vegetables in a large resealable plastic bag.

In a small bowl, whisk together the olive oil, rosemary, shallot, 1/2 teaspoon salt, and 1/4 teaspoon pepper. Add this mixture to the bag of vegetables. Allow the vegetables to marinate at room temperature for 10 to 15 minutes.

Remove the vegetables from the bag. Grill them directly over medium heat, turning once, until tender. The mushrooms will take 12 to 14 minutes, the bell peppers 10 to 12 minutes, the squashes 8 to 10 minutes, and the tomato 3 to 4 minutes. Transfer the grilled vegetables to a large platter and drizzle them with balsamic vinegar. Season with salt and pepper to taste.

Evenly spread the goat cheese on one side of 4 bread slices. Build the sandwiches with the grilled vegetables, interspersing the basil leaves as you build. Place the remaining bread slices on top. Serve warm or at room temperature.

EGGPLANT STACKS
WITH ROASTED CORN VINAIGRETTE

Fritz Sonnenschmidt

(Reprinted from Weber's Big Book of Grilling, Chronicle Books, 2001)

Sprinkling eggplant with salt will draw the bitter juices to the surface, which can then be blotted away. With the moisture drawn out, this popular late-summer vegetable will be left with a dense texture—perfect for the grill. – **Serves 4**

Vinaigrette

1 ear corn

1 red bell pepper

2 tablespoons finely chopped shallots

2 tablespoons balsamic vinegar

2 tablespoons coarsely chopped fresh basil

5 tablespoons extra virgin olive oil

8 (¼-inch-thick) tomato slices

Kosher salt

Freshly ground black pepper

Eggplant Stacks

12 eggplant slices, each about 4 inches in diameter and ½ inch thick

Kosher salt

Olive oil

Freshly ground black pepper

½ cup grated or sliced Asiago cheese

To make the vinaigrette: Soak the corn in water for 10 minutes. Grill the corn directly over medium heat, turning occasionally, until the husk is completely charred, 16 to 18 minutes. Remove and discard the charred husk and inner silks. Slice the kernels from the cob with a sharp knife and place them in a medium bowl.

Grill the bell pepper directly over medium heat, turning occasionally, until the skin is completely black and blistered, 10 to 12 minutes. Transfer the pepper to a paper bag, seal tightly, and let cool for 15 minutes. Remove the pepper, peel off and discard the skin. Remove the seeds and finely dice the pepper. Add the bell pepper to the corn along with the shallot, vinegar, basil, olive oil, and tomato slices. Season with salt and pepper to taste. Make sure vinaigrette covers the tomatoes.

To make the eggplant stacks: Rub both sides of the eggplant slices thoroughly with salt. Place them in a colander in the sink or over a plate for about 30 minutes to draw out the bitter juices. Rinse well and pat dry. Brush thoroughly with olive oil and season with salt and pepper.

Grill the eggplant slices directly over medium heat, turning once, until tender, 10 to 12 minutes.

Place 4 grilled eggplant slices on a small baking sheet. Top each with 1 tablespoon cheese and a marinated tomato slice. Repeat the layers, ending with an eggplant slice. Place the baking sheet on the grill directly over medium heat until the cheese melts, 2 to 3 minutes.

Place the stacks on individual plates. Spoon the vinaigrette on top and around the sides. Serve immediately.

CAPONATA BRUSCHETTA

Fritz Sonnenschmidt

(Reprinted from Weber's Big Book of Grilling, Chronicle Books, 2001)

Caponata is an Italian eggplant relish with a tantalizing sweet and sour taste. It can be served as a side dish, as a main course, or even as a sauce for pasta or rice. Here it is served as a hearty appetizer. Allow the mixture to rest for a few days, where the flavors will marry and become more intense. – **Serves 8**

1 eggplant (about 12 ounces), sliced crosswise ½ inch thick

Kosher salt

1 small yellow onion, sliced crosswise ½ inch thick

⅓ cup olive oil

1 tomato, seeded and roughly chopped

15 kalamata olives, pitted and finely chopped

2 tablespoons finely chopped fresh basil

1 tablespoon capers, drained

2 teaspoons balsamic vinegar

1 teaspoon finely chopped garlic

Freshly ground black pepper

8 slices Italian or other coarse country bread, about ½ inch thick and 4 inches wide

4 ounces fresh goat cheese, crumbled

Rub both sides of the eggplant slices thoroughly with salt. Allow them to sit in a colander placed in the sink or over a plate for about 30 minutes to draw out their bitter juices. Rinse the eggplant well and pat dry. Brush both sides of the eggplant and onion slices with the olive oil.

Grill the eggplant and onion slices directly over medium heat, turning once, until tender; 10 to 12 minutes total. Allow to cool. Coarsely chop the eggplant and onion slices and transfer to a medium bowl. Add the tomato, olives, basil, capers, vinegar, and garlic and mix well. Season with salt and pepper to taste.

Grill the bread slices directly over medium heat, turning once, until toasted, 2 to 3 minutes total. Divide the goat cheese evenly among the bread slices, spreading it with a knife. Spoon the caponata over the goat cheese, again dividing evenly. Serve at room temperature.

GRAPE LEAF-WRAPPED CAMEMBERT
WITH BACON AND ROASTED ONION TOPPING

Ted Reader

(Reprinted from Sticky Fingers and Tenderloins, Prentice-Hall Canada, 2001)

Grape leaves packed in brine can be bought in most large grocery stores or specialty food stores offering ethnic foods. Carefully unpack the leaves and rinse before wrapping the Camembert wheel. – **Serves 4**

8 slices smoked bacon

1 large onion, thinly sliced, plus

   1 onion, grilled and chopped

½ head fennel, very thinly sliced

2 scallions, chopped

1 tablespoon chopped fresh thyme

Salt and freshly cracked black

   pepper

Dash cider vinegar

1 small (125-gram) wheel

   Camembert

4 large grape leaves

2 tablespoons olive oil

French baguette slices, grilled

In a skillet over medium-high heat, fry the bacon until crisp. Drain on paper towels and let cool. Crumble the bacon.

In a large bowl, mix the onions, fennel, bacon, scallions, and thyme. Season to taste with salt, pepper, and a dash of cider vinegar.

Using a butter knife, scrape the white mold off the top of the Camembert. Season with cracked black pepper.

Lay the 4 grape leaves in a circle, overlapping slightly. Pat the top of the leaves dry with paper towels. Place the Camembert in the center of the leaves. Top with the onion mixture and spread it evenly. Wrap the leaves over the Camembert and press firmly to seal. If necessary, brush the edge of the leaves with olive oil to help form a seal.

Preheat the grill to medium-low heat.

Place the wrapped Camembert on the grill, onion topping side up, and grill for 8 to 12 minutes or until the cheese is soft. Press gently with a butter knife to check. Remove from the grill to a serving plate. Let cool for 2 minutes, and then carefully unwrap the leaves from the cheese. Spread or spoon the warm cheese over grilled baguette slices.

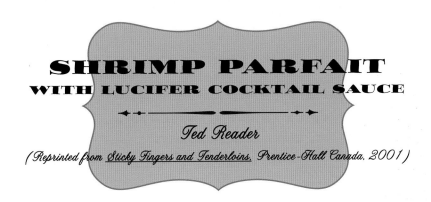

SHRIMP PARFAIT
WITH LUCIFER COCKTAIL SAUCE

Ted Reader

(Reprinted from Sticky Fingers and Tenderloins, Prentice-Hall Canada, 2001)

This appetizer will be a quick hit at any gathering. It is devilishly delightful. Have tortilla chips or crackers on the side to dig into the components of the parfait after the shrimp has been devoured. – **Serves 4**

Lucifer Cocktail Sauce

¹/₂ cup freshly grated horseradish

¹/₂ cup ketchup

¹/₂ cup chunky salsa

2 tablespoons freshly squeezed
   lemon juice

1 tablespoon white vinegar

2 teaspoons hot sauce

Salt, freshly ground black pepper,
   and Jack Daniel's sour mash
   whiskey to taste

Crab Salad

1 pound crabmeat

¹/₂ small red onion, diced

¹/₂ cup mayonnaise

2 scallions, chopped

1 tablespoon chopped fresh dill

1 tablespoon freshly squeezed
   lemon juice

1 tablespoon coarse-grain mustard

1 teaspoon white vinegar

1 dash hot sauce

Salt and freshly ground black
   pepper to taste

Guacamole

2 avocados, peeled and seeded

3 tablespoons freshly squeezed
   lemon juice

1 tablespoon chopped cilantro

¹/₂ small red onion, diced

2 cloves garlic, minced

3 scallions, finely chopped

Hot sauce, salt and freshly ground
   black pepper to taste

Grilled Tiger Shrimp

16 jumbo tiger shrimp, peeled
   and deveined, tails left on

3 tablespoons Bone Dust
   Barbecue Spice (recipe follows)

3 tablespoons olive oil

1 tablespoon chopped dill

Juice of 1 lime

Jack Daniel's to taste

To make the cocktail sauce: In a small bowl, stir together all the ingredients. Refrigerate until ready to serve. (Makes about 2 cups.)

To make the crab salad: In a bowl, stir together all the ingredients. Refrigerate until needed. (Makes about 2 cups.)

To make the guacamole: In a bowl, mash the avocados with a fork. Stir in the lemon juice, cilantro, onion, garlic, and scallions. Season with hot sauce, salt, and pepper. Cover and refrigerate. (Makes about 2 cups.)

To prepare the shrimp: In a bowl, toss the shrimp with barbecue spice, olive oil, dill, lime juice and Jack Daniel's. Marinate for 30 minutes.

Thread 4 shrimp each onto semicircular metal skewers.

Preheat grill to medium-high heat.

Place a large spoonful of cocktail sauce into each of 4 large parfait or milkshake glasses. Onto this, spoon some of the crab salad. Top with a dollop of guacamole. Repeat this layering until you reach the top of the glass.

Grill the skewered jumbo shrimp for 2 to 3 minutes per side or until opaque and just cooked through. Remove from the heat and balance a skewer of shrimp on top of each parfait. Serve immediately.

BONE DUST BARBECUE SPICE

Ted Reader

(Reprinted from The Sticks and Stones Cookbook, Macmillan Canada, 1999)

Makes approximately 2 ½ cups

$^1/_2$ cup paprika

$^1/_4$ cup chile powder

3 tablespoons salt

2 tablespoons ground coriander

2 tablespoons garlic powder

2 tablespoons granulated sugar

2 tablespoons curry powder

2 tablespoons dry hot mustard

1 tablespoon freshly ground black pepper

1 tablespoon ground basil

1 tablespoon ground thyme

1 tablespoon ground cumin

1 tablespoon cayenne

In a bowl, mix all ingredients together well. Store in a tightly sealed container.

ALUMINUM FOIL POTATOES
WITH SEXY SAUCES

Fritz Sonnenschmidt

These quick, simple sauces add a satisfying spark to the common potato. Slice the grilled potatoes thinly and arrange on a platter for a unique version of "chips and dip." – **Serves 8**

Dipping Sauce à la Russe

5 ounces sour cream

1/2 cup diced cooked red beets

1/4 cup mayonnaise

1/4 cup diced cucumbers

1 small onion, grated

1 small clove garlic, chopped or mashed

1 to 2 tablespoons grated horseradish

Herbal Dip

5 ounces heavy cream

3 ounces diced ham

1 tablespoon mild mustard

1 teaspoon freshly squeezed lemon juice

1 dash Worcestershire sauce

2 to 3 tablespoons chopped parsley and/or chives

Anchovy Dip

8 ounces small curd cottage cheese

1 tablespoon white wine

10 anchovy fillets, finely chopped or mashed

1 tablespoon chopped capers

1 sweet pickle, minced

2 tablespoons chopped chives

Salt and freshly ground black pepper to taste

2 tablespoons minced onions

Aluminum Foil Potatoes

8 (4-ounce) russet potatoes

1 tablespoon oil

1 teaspoon salt

2 tablespoons caraway seeds

In separate bowls, thoroughly combine the ingredients for each of the dips. Cover and refrigerate until ready to serve.

Wash and dry the potatoes well. Cut crosswise and place the potato disks on 8 aluminum foil squares. Brush the potatoes with oil.

In a small bowl, combine the salt and caraway seeds, and sprinkle this mixture over the potatoes. Place the foil sheets with the potatoes on the grill over medium heat (400 degrees F) and grill for 50 minutes. Serve immediately with the dipping sauces.

MARGARITA WINGS

Ted Reader

(Reprinted from Sticky Fingers and Tenderloins, Prentice-Hall Canada, 2001)

Every bit of juice counts. To get the most out of your lime, halve and squeeze. Then, flip the lime inside out and squeeze some more. You will be surprised just how much precious juice will continue to flow. – **Serves 4**

Margarita Wings

3 pounds whole jumbo chicken
  wings
3 tablespoons Bone Dust
  Barbecue Spice (see page 29)
3 tablespoons vegetable oil
3 tablespoons freshly squeezed
  lime juice
1/2 cup gold tequila
2 tablespoons hot sauce

Margarita Wing Sauce

1/2 cup honey
1/2 cup yellow mustard
1/4 cup coarse-grain mustard
1/2 cup freshly squeezed lime juice
3 tablespoons chopped fresh
  cilantro
2 tablespoons hot sauce
Salt, freshly ground black pepper,
  and Bone Dust Barbecue Spice
  (see page 29) to taste

Spicy Cheddar Cheese Dip

1 cup shredded Cheddar cheese
1 cup mayonnaise
1 cup ranch dressing
1/4 cup finely chopped onion
1 jalapeño, finely chopped
Juice of 1 lime

To prepare the wings: Tuck wing tips under the drummette to create a triangle. Place wings in a large bowl and toss with the remaining wing ingredients. Cover, refrigerate, and marinate for 4 to 6 hours.

To make the sauce: In a large bowl, whisk together all the ingredients and set aside.

To make the cheese dip: In a medium bowl, combine all the dip ingredients and mix thoroughly. Cover and refrigerate for 1 hour.

Preheat grill to medium heat.

Remove the chicken wings from the marinade and place on the grill. Cook for 15 to 20 minutes per side, turning every 5 to 6 minutes and basting with margarita sauce, or until fully cooked, golden brown, and crisp.

Carefully remove wings from the grill and serve with extra margarita sauce and spicy cheese dip.

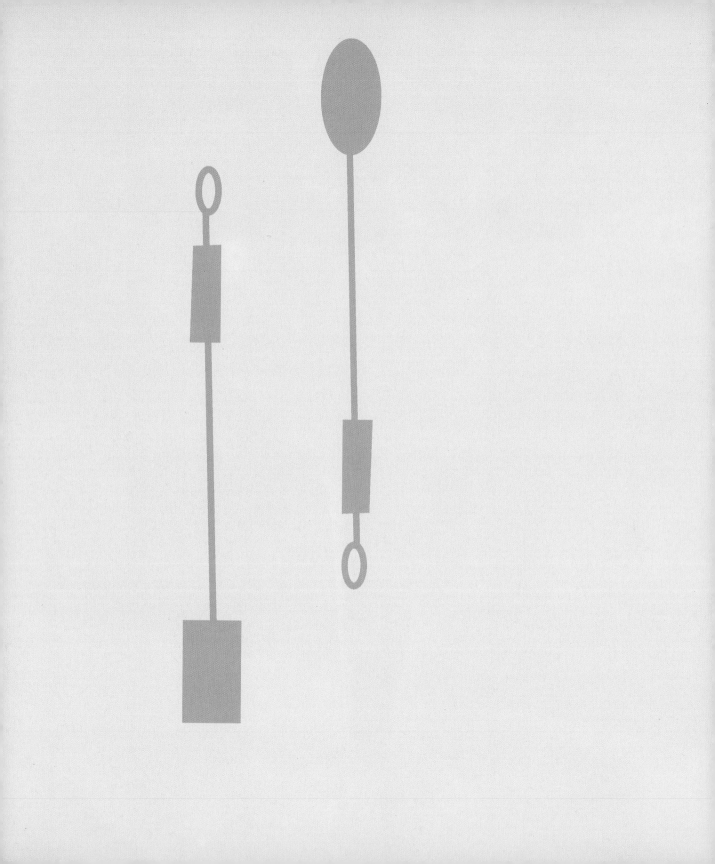

POULTRY

Chapter 2

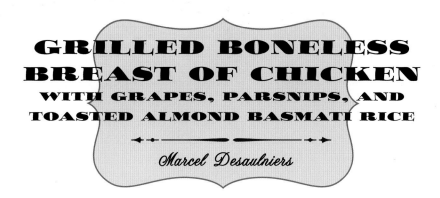

GRILLED BONELESS BREAST OF CHICKEN

WITH GRAPES, PARSNIPS, AND
TOASTED ALMOND BASMATI RICE

Marcel Desaulniers

The word *basmati* means fragrant in Hindi and refers to the intense flavor and aroma of this long-grain rice. The addition of fruits and nuts lends a delightful taste and texture to an already delicious accompaniment. – **Serves 4**

4 (5- to 6-ounce) boneless, skinless chicken breasts

2 tablespoons freshly squeezed lemon juice

2 tablespoons plus ¼ cup Sauvignon Blanc or other dry white wine

Salt and freshly ground black pepper

2 teaspoons peanut oil

1 cup white basmati rice

1 ³/4 cups hot chicken stock

2 tablespoons rice wine

¹/2 cup toasted, sliced almonds

3 tablespoons butter

1 cup red seedless grapes, cut in half

1 Red Delicious apple, sliced ¹/4 inch thick

4 parsnips (about 12 ounces), ends trimmed, peeled, and cut into sticks 3 inches long and ¹/4 inch thick

¹/2 cup raisins

Trim any excess fat from the chicken breasts. Sprinkle both sides of the chicken breasts with the lemon juice and 2 tablespoons white wine, and then season each side with salt and pepper. Wrap each breast individually in plastic wrap and refrigerate for at least 2 hours (and up to 24 hours).

Heat the peanut oil in a 3-quart saucepan over medium-high heat. When hot, add the basmati rice and stir to coat with oil. Season with salt and pepper, and stir to combine. Add the hot chicken stock and the rice wine, and stir to blend. Raise the heat to high and bring to a boil. As soon as the stock boils, cover the saucepan and lower the heat to medium. Cook the rice until tender, about 15 minutes. Remove the rice from the heat and stir in the toasted almonds. Keep the rice warm while grilling the chicken.

Grill the chicken breasts over medium heat for 2¹/2 to 3 minutes on each side.

Layer 2 foot-long pieces of aluminum foil over each other for strength. In the center of the foil, place the butter, grape halves, apple slices, parsnip sticks, and raisins. Fold and seal two sides of the foil over the fruit and parsnips, and then fold and seal one end. Pour the remaining ¹/4 cup white wine into the open end and seal to make a pouch. Place the pouch in the grill directly over medium heat for 5 to 6 minutes.

Place an equal amount of rice on each of 4 plates. Place a chicken breast on each bed of rice. Sprinkle an equal amount of roasted parsnips and fruit over each chicken breast. Serve immediately.

GRILLED MARINATED CHICKEN
WITH CAULIFLOWER, CELERY, RED ONION, AND QUINOA SALAD AND HERBED YOGURT DRESSING

Marcel Desaulniers

Quinoa is an ancient and extremely nutritional grain—a virtual protein powerhouse full of vitamins and minerals. This super-grain is enjoying a renaissance in this country and for good reason—it exudes a light, delicate taste and a soft fluffy texture. Buckwheat or barley can be substituted for quinoa. – **Serves 4**

2 cups plain low-fat yogurt
1/4 cup freshly squeezed lemon juice
1/4 cup chopped fresh flat-leaf parsley
2 tablespoons chopped fresh dill
2 tablespoons chopped fresh mint
Salt and freshly ground black pepper to taste
2 (2 1/2-pound) chickens, halved
1 large head white cauliflower (about 2 pounds), trimmed, cored, cut into small florets, and sliced 1/4 inch thick

4 stalks celery (about 1/2 pound), trimmed and cut diagonally into strips 2 inches long and 1/4 inch thick
1 large red onion (about 1/2 pound), peeled and thinly sliced
2 cups dry white wine
1/2 cup white wine vinegar
4 cloves garlic, peeled
1 lemon, cut into 1/2-inch pieces, seeds removed
1 tablespoon whole black peppercorns
1 bay leaf

1/2 cup extra virgin olive oil
4 cups vegetable stock
1 teaspoon sea salt
2 cups toasted quinoa
3 tablespoons safflower oil
1/4 pound watercress, trimmed, washed, and dried

In a 3-quart nonreactive bowl, whisk together the yogurt, lemon juice, parsley, dill, and mint until thoroughly combined. Season with salt and pepper. Place 1 cup of the yogurt mixture in a noncorrosive, covered container, and refrigerate until needed to dress the salads.

Season the chicken halves with salt and pepper, and then coat with the remaining yogurt mixture. Wrap each half individually in plastic wrap and refrigerate for several hours before grilling.

Place the sliced cauliflower, celery, and red onion in a 5-quart saucepan. Set aside.

In a 3-quart saucepan over medium-high heat, heat the white wine, white wine vinegar, garlic, lemon, peppercorns, and bay leaf. Bring this marinade to a boil, and then adjust the heat and simmer for 10 minutes. Strain the marinade over the vegetables in the 5-quart saucepan.

Over medium-high heat, heat the vegetables in the marinade. As soon as the marinade begins to boil, remove from the heat and transfer the vegetables along with the marinade to a 7-quart nonreactive bowl. Add the extra virgin olive oil and combine with a rubber spatula. Season with salt and pepper. Immediately cover tightly with plastic wrap, and refrigerate at least 1 hour before serving. (The marinated vegetables may be refrigerated for 2 to 3 days in a covered, non-reactive container.)

Heat the vegetable stock with the sea salt in a 3-quart saucepan over medium-high heat. Bring to a boil. Add the toasted quinoa and return to a boil. Lower the heat to medium-low and simmer, covered, for 15 minutes, until most of the liquid has evaporated. Transfer the quinoa to a 5-quart stainless-steel bowl. Add the safflower oil and combine with a rubber spatula. Season with salt and pepper. Cool, uncovered, at room temperature for 1 hour, stirring occasionally.

Grill the chicken breasts over medium heat for 25 minutes. Turn the chicken halves as necessary to prevent overcharring. Remove the chicken from the grill.

Divide and arrange the watercress, stem ends toward the center, in a ring, with the leaf ends near the outside edge of four 10- to 12-inch room-temperature soup or pasta plates. Evenly divide the quinoa in a ring inside the ring of watercress on each plate. With a slotted spoon, portion an equal amount of marinated cauliflower salad in the center of the quinoa ring. Dress each salad with 3 to 4 tablespoons of dressing. Place a chicken half on each. Serve immediately.

GRILLED TURKEY MEAT LOAF
WITH HAND-CUT FRIES

Fritz Sonnenschmidt

(Hand-Cut French Fries with Spicy Ketchup reprinted from Weber's Big Book of Grilling, Chronicle Books, 2001)

Dip your hands in a bowl of cold water before forming the turkey loaves. – **Serves 4**

Turkey Meat Loaf

1 hard roll or 2 slices white bread, cubed and toasted

3 ounces milk, warmed

1 tablespoon butter

1/2 yellow onion, thinly sliced

1 clove garlic, minced

1 pound ground turkey

1 egg

1 teaspoon mustard

1 tablespoon chopped parsley

1/2 teaspoon chopped marjoram

1/4 teaspoon paprika

Salt and freshly ground black pepper

Vegetable oil

Hand-Cut French Fries with Spicy Ketchup

1/4 cup ketchup

1/2 teaspoon chile sauce

1/2 teaspoon balsamic vinegar

2 russet potatoes, about 8 ounces each

1 tablespoon olive oil

1 tablespoon minced garlic

1/2 teaspoon kosher salt

1/2 teaspoon freshly ground black pepper

To make meat loaf: In a small bowl, soak the cubed and toasted roll or bread in warm milk. In a small skillet, heat the butter and sauté the onions and garlic for 1 minute. Remove the pan from the heat and allow to cool. Squeeze bread to remove the liquid. In a large bowl, combine the ground turkey with the bread, egg, sautéed onions and garlic, mustard, parsley, marjoram, paprika, salt, and pepper, and mix well. (Do not overmix meat loaf mixture or it will become tough.) Mold into 8 balls and flatten out. Brush the loaves with vegetable oil. Grill over medium-high heat approximately 4 to 5 minutes on each side.

To make the ketchup and french fries: In a small bowl, mix together the ketchup, chile sauce, and balsamic vinegar. Set aside.

Scrub the potatoes under cold running water and dry thoroughly, but do not peel. Cut lengthwise into 1/2-inch-thick slices, then cut the slices into 1/4-inch wedges. Place the wedges in a medium bowl and toss with the olive oil, garlic, salt and pepper.

Place the wedges on the grill over medium heat, being careful not to let them drop through the openings. Grill the potatoes until golden brown, turning once, about 10 minutes. For extra-crispy fries, open the grill and cook for an additional 1 to 2 minutes, turning once.

Place the meat loaves and the french fries on a large serving platter and serve immediately with the ketchup.

TURKEY DRUMSTICKS
SLATHERED WITH BARBECUE SAUCE
AND POTATO HASH

Fritz Sonnenschmidt

Cooking turkey on the grill is becoming an increasingly popular alternative to roasting in the oven. If you don't have a rotisserie, you can place the well-oiled drumsticks in the center of the grill, with only the two outer burners on. This indirect cooking method will ensure an evenly browned and mouthwatering product. – **Serves 4**

Barbecue Sauce

2 tablespoons olive oil

1/2 cup finely chopped red onion

2 cloves garlic, finely chopped

1/4 cup dry red wine

1/4 cup ketchup

1/4 cup steak sauce

1 1/2 tablespoons Worcestershire sauce

1 teaspoon dried sage

1/2 teaspoon freshly ground black pepper

Turkey Drumsticks

Vegetable oil

4 turkey drumsticks (about 1 pound each)

Potato Hash

Vegetable oil

8 russet potatoes

2 tablespoons olive oil

1 onion, finely diced

1 clove garlic, finely diced

3 ounces pancetta, cubed

1/2 pound ground turkey

1/4 cup chopped chives

1 teaspoon salt

Freshly ground black pepper

1/4 cup grated Swiss cheese

2 tablespoons butter

To make the barbecue sauce: In a medium saucepan over medium-high heat, warm the olive oil. Add the onion and garlic. Cook, stirring occasionally, until soft, about 5 minutes. Add the red wine, ketchup, steak sauce, Worcestershire sauce, sage, and pepper. Bring to a boil, reduce the heat to a simmer, and cook for 5 minutes. Remove from the heat.

To make the drumsticks: Lightly brush the grill grate with vegetable oil. Lightly coat the turkey drumsticks with the barbecue sauce. Grill them indirectly over medium heat, turning and basting with the barbecue sauce every 30 minutes, until the juices run clear and the internal temperature is 180 degrees F, for a total of 1 1/2 to 2 hours. Remove from the grill and keep warm.

To make potato hash: Preheat grill to medium-high heat. Brush 8 large aluminum foil squares with vegetable oil. Wash potatoes and dry. Grill for 40 minutes over indirect heat. Allow to cool. Cube the potatoes. Heat olive oil in a large skillet and sauté onion and garlic for 2 minutes. Add pancetta, potatoes, ground turkey, and chives. Sauté for 5 to 6 minutes. Add salt and pepper.

Place potato hash in a well-oiled medium casserole dish. Sprinkle with grated Swiss cheese

and top with a dollop of butter. Place on the upper shelf of the grill for 10 minutes. Remove from the grill.

Place the turkey drumsticks and potato hash on a platter and serve immediately.

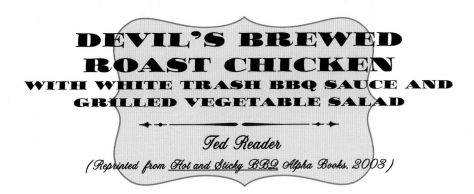

DEVIL'S BREWED ROAST CHICKEN
WITH WHITE TRASH BBQ SAUCE AND GRILLED VEGETABLE SALAD

Ted Reader

(Reprinted from Hot and Sticky BBQ, Alpha Books, 2003)

Roasting a whole chicken is a great way to please the whole family. You get your choice of white or dark meat. – **Serves 4 to 6**

Grilled Vegetable Salad

2 large zucchini, cut in half
  lengthwise
3 large tomatoes, cut in half
1 large onion, cut in half
$1/2$ cup cider vinegar
$1/2$ cup olive oil
Salt, freshly ground black pepper,
  and Bone Dust Barbecue Spice
  (see page 29) to taste
1 small log goat cheese, crumbled

White Trash BBQ Sauce

2 tablespoons butter
1 tablespoon vegetable oil
6 to 8 cloves garlic, chopped
1 tablespoon each chopped fresh
  rosemary, parsley, and thyme
1 cup ranch dressing
1 cup mayonnaise
$1/2$ cup whipping cream
Salt, black pepper, hot sauce

Roast Chicken

2 (3- to 4-pound) chickens
$1/2$ cup Bone Dust Barbecue Spice
  (see page 29)
2 (375-ml) cans lager or ale
$1/4$ cup ($1/2$ stick) butter
$1/4$ cup hot sauce
2 tablespoons freshly squeezed
  lemon juice

To make the salad: Preheat the grill to medium-high heat. Grill the vegetables for 10 to 12 minutes to soften and lightly char. Remove from heat and cool slightly. Chop the vegetables in big chunks and add the cider vinegar, olive oil, salt, pepper, and barbecue spice. Add the goat cheese and gently mix. Set the salad aside.

To prepare the barbecue sauce: In a medium saucepan, sauté the butter, oil and garlic for 1 to 2 minutes. Stir in the rosemary, parsley, and thyme, ranch dressing, mayonnaise, and cream. Bring to a boil over medium heat, stirring constantly. Season with salt, pepper, and hot sauce. Set aside.

To prepare the chicken: Rub the chickens inside and out with the barbecue spice, pushing the spice firmly onto the birds so it adheres.

Place a foil pie plate inside another foil pie plate. Place 1 beer can on the pie plates. Place 1 chicken over the beer can so the can is in the bird's cavity and the bird is standing upright. Repeat with 2 more pie plates, the remaining can of beer, and the other chicken.

In a small saucepan over medium heat, melt the butter. Stir in the hot sauce and lemon juice. Heat, stirring, until well blended.

Place the chickens on the pie plates on the grill. Close the lid and grill the chickens for 50 to 60 minutes, or until fully cooked and golden brown, basting liberally with the sauce. (Insert a meat thermometer into the thigh; it should read 160 degrees F.)

Remove the chicken from the grill and serve with vegetable salad and barbecue sauce.

GRILLED CHICKEN AND VEGETABLE FRIED RICE

Ted Reader

Hoisin is a sweet and spicy sauce made of a mixture of soybeans, garlic, chile peppers, and various spices. It is a flavoring agent and condiment commonly used in Chinese cooking. In this recipe, hoisin is used to season the tender grilled chicken before it is added to the fried rice. **– Serves 6**

1 cup honey

1 cup hoisin sauce

4 boneless, skinless chicken breasts

1 each red, yellow and green peppers, cut into chunks

1 red onion, cut into chunks

2 cups button mushrooms, quartered

1 cup corn kernels

2 tablespoons Bone Dust Barbecue Spice (see page 29)

2 tablespoons plus ¼ cup soy sauce

1 tablespoon olive oil

3 tablespoons peanut oil

6 slices bacon, cooked

12 large shrimp, cooked

3 cups cooked rice

Preheat grill to medium-high heat.

In a small bowl, mix the honey and the hoisin sauce together and set aside.

Grill chicken for 8 to 10 minutes or until fully cooked. Baste liberally with honey hoisin sauce. Remove the chicken from the grill and allow to cool. Slice into chunks and set aside.

In a large foil bag, place the peppers, onion, mushrooms, corn, barbecue spice, 2 tablespoons soy sauce and olive oil. Seal well and place the bag on the grill. Grill for 15 to 20 minutes, turning twice. Remove from grill and set aside.

Fit the grill with the wok attachment. To the wok add the peanut oil and allow to heat up. Toss in the bacon, shrimp, and grilled chicken and stir well for 2 minutes. Add the rice and stir for 2 more minutes. Add in the grilled vegetables from the foil pouch and the remaining ¼ cup soy sauce. Remove from the heat and drizzle with any extra honey hoisin sauce. Serve immediately with the rice.

GRILLED THANKSGIVING BBQ TURKEY CASSEROLE

Ted Reader

This hearty casserole is a fun and tasty alternative to the traditional Thanksgiving turkey. The abundance of ingredients that go into this dish makes for an impressive feast of the senses. – **Serves 8 to 10**

1 (4- to 5-pound) fresh boneless turkey breast

1/4 cup Bone Dust Barbecue Spice (see page 29) plus extra to taste

1 cup barbecue sauce

1/4 cup maple syrup

1 tablespoon brown sugar

1/4 cup olive oil

2 white onions, diced

1 red onion, diced

2 carrots, peeled and lightly blanched

3 cups sliced mushrooms

Salt and freshly ground black pepper

1 loaf sliced white bread, cut in large squares

3 stalks celery, diced

8 slices thick sliced bacon, diced and parfried

1 cup chopped dried apricots

3 cloves garlic, minced

1/2 cup (1 stick) butter, melted

1/4 cup milk

1 tablespoon each fresh savory and sage

2 cups cubed Gruyère cheese

Rub the turkey with the barbecue spice and place in a smoker for 6 to 7 hours at 225 degrees F. Remove the turkey from the smoker and allow to cool. Shred the turkey into a medium bowl. In a small bowl, mix 1/2 cup barbecue sauce, maple syrup, and brown sugar and add to the shredded turkey and set aside.

Heat the olive oil over medium-high heat in a large skillet. Add half the diced white onion, the red onion, carrots, and mushrooms and season to taste with salt, pepper, and barbecue spice. Cook for 5 to 6 minutes to reduce the moisture and remove from heat.

In a large bowl, place the bread, the remaining white onion, celery, bacon, apricots, garlic, butter, milk, herbs, and cheese. Mix this stuffing well with your hands and season to taste with salt and pepper. Set aside.

In a deep-dish casserole or large foil lasagna pan, place the mushroom and onion mixture and spread evenly on the bottom followed by the smoked turkey with barbecue sauce. Crumble the stuffing evenly over the top and cover loosely with aluminum foil.

Preheat the grill to medium.

Place the casserole in the grill for 20 minutes with the lid closed. Remove the foil and grill for 45 minutes to 1 hour, until it is hot throughout and the top is browned nicely. Rotate once during cooking. Remove from grill and allow to rest for 5 minutes before serving with the barbecue gravy.

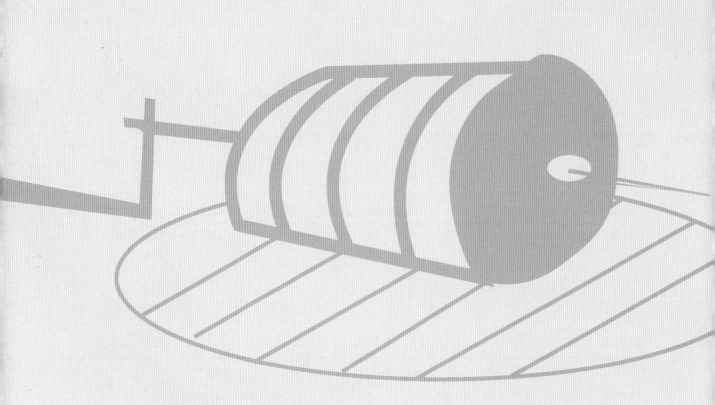

MEAT

Chapter 3

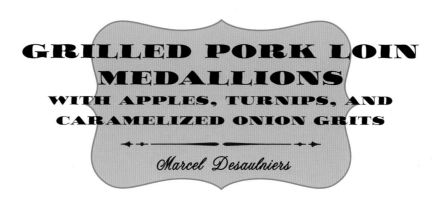

GRILLED PORK LOIN MEDALLIONS
WITH APPLES, TURNIPS, AND CARAMELIZED ONION GRITS

Marcel Desaulniers

The essence of comfort food lies in a dish such as this. Soul-satisfying flavors emerge from the savory pork and the winning combination of apples and turnips. Creamy grits accented with caramelized onions round out this nurturing experience. – **Serves 4**

2 tablespoons peanut oil

2 tablespoons cider vinegar

1 tablespoon peanut butter

1 tablespoon light corn syrup

1 1/2 pounds well-trimmed boneless pork loin, cut into 1/2-inch-thick medallions

1 tablespoon vegetable oil

2 onions, thinly sliced

1 teaspoon salt plus extra to taste

1/2 teaspoon freshly ground black pepper plus extra to taste

1 small white turnip, peeled, and cut into thin strips

1 tablespoon freshly squeezed lemon juice

1 Red Delicious apple

1 cup heavy cream

2 cups chicken stock

1 cup half-and-half

2 tablespoons butter

1 cup stone-ground grits

In a 3-quart bowl, whisk together the peanut oil, cider vinegar, peanut butter, and light corn syrup. Add the pork medallions and turn each a few times to coat with the marinade. Divide into 4 portions of 4 medallions. Wrap each portion individually in plastic wrap and refrigerate until needed.

Heat the vegetable oil in a nonstick sauté pan over medium heat. When the oil is hot, add the onions and season to taste with salt and pepper. Sauté the onions until they are evenly browned, adding 1 to 2 tablespoons water at a time to wash down the accumulated caramel. (This should be done 4 to 6 times during the cooking.) Stir frequently while the onions are browning, for 30 to 35 minutes. Keep the caramelized onions warm while completing the recipe.

Blanch the turnip strips in boiling salted water for about 1 minute. Transfer to ice water and let cool. Drain thoroughly.

Combine 2 cups water with 1 tablespoon lemon juice. Core, quarter, and slice the unpeeled apple, placing the slices in the acidulated water as you go along.

Heat the heavy cream in a 3-quart saucepan over medium heat. When the cream begins to simmer, lower the heat so that the cream continues to simmer (do not boil) for 10 minutes.

Drain the apple slices in a colander, rinse them under cold running water, and shake dry. Add the apple slices and the blanched turnip strips to the cream. Continue to heat on low while preparing the grits.

Heat the chicken stock, half-and-half, butter, 1 teaspoon salt, and 1/2 teaspoon freshly ground black pepper in a 3-quart saucepan over medium heat. Bring the mixture to a boil, then add the grits in a slow, steady stream while stirring constantly with a rigid wire whisk. Continue to cook over low heat, stirring constantly, for 8 to 10 minutes until thick. Remove the grits mixture from the heat and add the caramelized onions, stirring until incorporated. Keep warm while grilling the pork medallions.

Season the pork medallions with salt and pepper and grill over medium-low heat for 3 1/2 to 4 minutes on each side.

Divide the caramelized grits among 4 warm plates. Spoon the apple, turnips, and cream over the grits. Top with the pork loin medallions and serve immediately.

GRILLED LAMB LOIN
WITH ONIONS, POTATOES, CABBAGE, AND HERBS

Marcel Desaulniers

This untraditional stew reflects the satisfying flavors of Ireland. The heartiness of meat and potatoes will satisfy almost any palate. Add the reserved herb mixture at the very end to enhance the subtle flavors. – **Serves 4**

1 lamb loin, $^1/_2$ to $^3/_4$ inch thick
2 tablespoons extra virgin olive oil
1 tablespoon chopped fresh parsley
1 tablespoon chopped fresh rosemary
1 tablespoon chopped fresh thyme
Salt and freshly ground black pepper

2 tablespoons butter
2 large onions, sliced
1 stalk celery, chopped
1 small parsnip, chopped
1 $^1/_4$ pounds green cabbage, discolored and tough outer leaves removed, cored, quartered, and sliced $^1/_4$ inch thick

3 cups hot chicken stock
1 pound potatoes, peeled, cut into 1-inch cubes, and covered with cold water

Coat the lamb loin with the olive oil. In a small bowl, combine the parsley, rosemary, and thyme. Sprinkle half of the herb mixture over the lamb. Season with salt and pepper. Set the remaining herbs aside for later use.

Heat 1 tablespoon of the butter and 1 tablespoon water in a 5-quart saucepan over medium-high heat. When hot, add half of the chopped onion, all the celery and parsnips, and half of the cabbage. Season with salt and pepper and sauté until hot, about 5 minutes Add the hot chicken stock. Drain the potatoes, rinse them with cold water, and add them to the saucepan. Bring the mixture to a boil, then reduce the heat and simmer slowly for 30 minutes.

Purée the hot potato and cabbage mixture in a food processor fitted with a metal blade. Return the puréed mixture to the saucepan and bring to a simmer.

Heat the remaining tablespoon of butter with 1 tablespoon water in a large nonstick sauté pan over medium-high heat. When hot, add the remaining sliced onions, season with salt and pepper, and sauté for 3 minutes. Add the remaining raw cabbage, season with salt and pepper, and sauté for 5 to 6 minutes. When the cabbage and onions are hot, combine with the puréed potato and cabbage mixture, and keep very hot while grilling the lamb.

Season the lamb with salt and pepper and grill over medium-high heat for 4 to 5 minutes on each side, depending upon the desired degree of doneness. Remove from the grill and allow to rest for 5 minutes before slicing.

Divide the braised vegetables among 4 warm soup or pasta plates, top each with a slice of grilled lamb. Sprinkle with some of the remaining chopped herbs, and serve immediately.

GRILLED VEAL CHOP
WITH ROOT VEGETABLES AND ROSEMARY CREAM

Marcel Desaulniers

Veal is naturally lean and exceptionally versatile. It can be cooked in a variety of ways, and its distinctive flavor absorbs seasonings easily. Rosemary, a key ingredient in this recipe, adds an assertive aroma to this nourishing meal. – **Serves 4**

1 parsnip, trimmed and peeled

1 turnip, trimmed and peeled

1 carrot, trimmed and peeled

1 rutabaga, trimmed and peeled

2 tablespoons butter

2 tablespoons chopped fresh rosemary

Salt and freshly ground black pepper

1/2 cup heavy cream

4 (12-ounce) veal loin chops

2 tablespoons extra virgin olive oil

Slice each vegetable into 1/4-inch-thick slices, then into strips 2 to 2 1/2 inches long. Bring 3 quarts of salted water to a boil in a large saucepan over medium-high heat. Blanch each vegetable separately in the same pot: parsnips for 1 1/2 minutes, turnips for 1 1/2 minutes, carrots for 2 1/2 minutes, and then the rutabaga for 2 1/2 minutes. After blanching each vegetable, transfer them to ice water. When cold, remove them from the water and drain thoroughly. Refrigerate until needed.

Heat the butter and 1 tablespoon water in a large nonstick pan over medium heat. When hot, add the prepared vegetables and 1 tablespoon of the rosemary. Season with salt and pepper and sauté for 5 to 6 minutes, until hot. Add the heavy cream and heat until the cream begins to simmer. Adjust the seasoning with salt and pepper and keep warm while grilling the veal chops.

Brush the veal chops with the olive oil. Season liberally with salt and pepper and sprinkle each on both sides with the remaining 1 tablespoon rosemary. Grill the chops over medium-high heat for 4 to 6 minutes on each side, depending upon the desired degree of doneness.

Divide the root vegetables among 4 warm plates and top each with a veal chop. Serve immediately.

GRILLED SZECHUAN-STYLE SKIRT STEAK

WITH WHITE MUSHROOMS, SPINACH, AND BLACK PEPPER DRESSING

Marcel Desaulniers

Szechuan is well known for its spicy contributions to Chinese cuisine, which inspire this zesty steak recipe. Szechuan pepper has a distinctive flavor and fragrance. It can be found in Asian markets and specialty stores in whole or powdered form. – **Serves 4**

Szechuan-Style Skirt Steak

1 tablespoon Szechuan
  peppercorns
1/4 cup soy sauce
1 tablespoon sugar
1 tablespoon minced fresh ginger
1 tablespoon sesame oil
1/4 cup olive oil
1 teaspoon salt
4 (6- to 8-ounce) skirt steaks

Pepper Dressing

2 large egg yolks
1 tablespoon lemon juice
1 1/2 cups vegetable oil
1/4 cup water
3 tablespoons grated Parmesan
  cheese
1 tablespoon whole black
  peppercorns, coarsely cracked
1 1/2 teaspoons sugar

1 teaspoon Dijon mustard
1 anchovy, minced
Salt and freshly ground black pepper

Spinach and Mushrooms

1 (10-ounce) bag curly spinach,
  washed and spun dry
1/2 pound white button mushrooms,
  stems trimmed, and quartered
2 scallions, trimmed and thinly
  sliced (for garnish)

To marinate the skirt steaks: Toast the peppercorns in a sauté pan over medium heat, about 5 minutes. Cool them to room temperature before coarsely grinding in a spice or coffee grinder.

In a stainless steel bowl, whisk together the soy sauce and sugar until the sugar has dissolved. Add the ginger and sesame oil and combine. Add the olive oil in a slow, steady stream while whisking until emulsified and thick. Add the ground peppercorns and the salt and combine. Add the steaks and turn to coat with marinade. Cover the bowl with plastic wrap and refrigerate for at least 2 hours (and up to 24 hours).

To make the dressing: Combine the egg yolks and lemon juice in a stainless steel bowl. Whisk vigorously until they are light in color and frothy, about 1 minute. Continue to whisk this

mixture while slowly drizzling in the vegetable oil. Add the water, Parmesan, cracked black pepper, sugar, mustard, and anchovy. Stir to incorporate. Season with salt and pepper. Cover with plastic wrap and refrigerate until needed.

To grill the skirt steaks: Remove the skirt steaks from the marinade. Grill over medium heat for 2 1/2 to 3 minutes on each side for rare to medium rare. Remove from the grill.

To assemble: Portion the spinach leaves onto 4 plates. Top the greens with an equal amount of mushrooms and dress each salad with 4 tablespoons of dressing. Place a grilled skirt steak onto the spinach and mushrooms. Garnish with sliced scallions. Serve immediately.

GRILLED PORK TENDERLOIN
WITH SHRIMP, BROCCOLI, COUNTRY HAM, AND
TOASTED PEANUT BUTTER

Marcel Desaulniers

This dish, infused with Southern flavors, is topped with a unique rendition of "peanut butter." To guarantee a satisfying crunch to the finishing touch, pop the shelled peanuts in a hot oven for a few minutes before adding to the recipe. – **Serves 4**

1 1/2 pounds pork tenderloin
3 tablespoons peanut oil
2 tablespoons honey
1 tablespoon dry mustard
2 teaspoons sea salt
1 teaspoon cayenne pepper

1 pound large (16–20) large
 shrimp, peeled and deveined
1/2 cup toasted unsalted shelled
 peanuts, finely chopped
1/2 cup (1 stick) butter, softened
Salt and freshly ground black
 pepper

1 large bunch broccoli (about 1 1/2
 pounds), stems trimmed, and
 cut into florets
1/4 pound cooked salt-cured ham,
 cut into strips 1 1/2 inches long
 and 1/8 inch wide

Thoroughly trim the fat and membrane from the pork tenderloin. Cut the tenderloin into 4 equal portions. Place the pork, 1 portion at a time, between 2 sheets of lightly oiled aluminum foil or parchment paper. Uniformly flatten each tenderloin to about 3/4-inch thickness with a meat cleaver or the bottom of a sauté pan.

In a 3-quart bowl, whisk together the peanut oil, honey, dry mustard, sea salt, and cayenne pepper. Add the pork tenderloin and turn each a few times to coat with the marinade. Remove the pork from the marinade, allowing excess marinade to drip back into the bowl. Wrap each portion individually in plastic wrap and refrigerate until ready to grill. Add the shrimp to the remaining marinade and toss until well coated. Remove the shrimp from the marinade. Skewer the shrimp onto 4 skewers. Cover them with plastic wrap and refrigerate until ready to grill.

Combine the chopped peanuts with the softened butter. Season with salt and pepper and mix thoroughly. Cover this "peanut butter" with plastic wrap and set aside at room temperature.

Grill the pork tenderloin portions over medium heat for 3 to 3 1/2 minutes on each side. Keep warm until you are ready to serve.

Grill the shrimp over low heat for about 2 minutes on each side. Remove the shrimp from the skewers and keep warm.

Bring 2 quarts of lightly salted water to a boil in a 3-quart saucepan over medium-high heat. Add the broccoli and cook until tender but still crunchy, about 2 1/2 to 3 minutes. Drain in a colander.

Arrange the broccoli florets in a ring, stems toward the center, along the outer edges of 4 warm plates. Place a pork tenderloin in the center of each ring and grilled shrimp and ham around each pork tenderloin. Top each portion of pork with 1 tablespoon peanut butter. Serve immediately.

GRILLED BISON FILLET
WITH ARUGULA, GARBANZO BEANS, AND SPICY PEANUT SAUCE

Marcel Desaulniers

Bison fillet is rapidly gaining popularity in fine food circles. Not only is the meat nutritionally lower in fat, cholesterol, and calories than most other meats, it has an exceptionally richer and sweeter flavor than beef. If bison is not readily available in your area, any tender cut of beef can be easily substituted. – **Serves 4**

Garbanzo Bean Salad

$3/4$ cup dried garbanzo beans, washed, picked over, and soaked for 12 hours in 1 pint of cold water

1 teaspoon salt plus extra to taste

2 plum tomatoes, washed, cored, and chopped into $1/4$-inch pieces

2 tablespoons balsamic vinegar

1 tablespoon fresh lemon juice

$1/2$ cup peanut oil

1 tablespoon stemmed coarsely chopped flat-leaf parsley

Freshly ground black pepper

Spicy Peanut Sauce

1 tablespoon peanut oil

2 tablespoons minced shallot

1 tablespoon minced jalapeño pepper

1 cup chicken stock

2 teaspoons fresh lemon juice

$1/2$ cup creamy peanut butter

1 tablespoon tightly packed dark brown sugar

1 or 2 pinches cayenne pepper

Grilled Bison Fillets

$1/4$ teaspoon curry powder

$1/4$ teaspoon freshly ground black pepper

$1/4$ teaspoon salt

4 (5- to 6-ounce) bison fillets

1 tablespoon peanut oil

$1/4$ pound stemmed, washed, and dried arugula

To make the salad: Drain the soaked garbanzo beans in a colander. Rinse them in cold water, and drain thoroughly before cooking.

Bring 2 pints water and 1 teaspoon salt to a boil in a small saucepan over high heat. Add the beans, adjust the heat, and simmer the beans until tender, about 45 minutes. Drain the beans in a colander, and then transfer to a stainless steel bowl. Add the chopped plum tomatoes.

In a separate bowl, vigorously whisk together the balsamic vinegar and lemon juice. Add the peanut oil in a slow, steady stream while whisking until incorporated. Add to the beans and tomatoes, along with the parsley. Using a rubber spatula, stir the ingredients until combined. Season with salt and pepper. Cover the bowl with plastic wrap and set aside for up to 3 hours at room temperature.

To make the peanut sauce: Heat the peanut oil in a small saucepan over medium heat. When hot, add the shallots and the jalapeño. Sauté for 30 seconds. Add the chicken stock and lemon juice and bring to a boil. Remove the pan from the heat. Add the peanut butter, brown sugar, and cayenne pepper, and whisk vigorously until smooth.

To prepare the bison: In a small bowl, combine the curry powder, ground black pepper, and salt. Generously season both sides of each bison fillet with the seasoning mix. Cover the fillets with plastic wrap and refrigerate until needed.

Preheat the grill to medium-high heat. Remove the bison from the refrigerator and brush each fillet with peanut oil. Grill the fillets for about 2 minutes on each side for rare to medium-rare doneness.

Divide the arugula leaves onto 4 plates. Stir the garbanzo bean mixture. Use a slotted spoon to divide the beans evenly onto the arugula leaves on each plate. Place a bison fillet on top of the beans. Finish by drizzling about 2 tablespoons peanut sauce over each. Serve immediately.

GRILLED SAUSAGE, PORTOBELLO MUSHROOMS, AND VEGETABLES

WITH MARINATED FRENCH LENTILS

Marcel Desaulniers

Lentils are an ancient crop and are a staple of protein for many cultures all over the world. These low-fat legumes are considered a "wonder food" because they are high in carbohydrates, protein, and fiber. This delicious recipe further proves just how wonderful they are. – **Serves 4**

1 1/2 cups French green lentils, picked over, washed, and drained	1/4 cup finely chopped celery	4 large portobello mushroom caps (about 5 ounces each), stems removed
1 teaspoon salt plus extra to taste	Freshly ground black pepper	
1 tablespoon plus 1/2 cup safflower oil	1/2 cup red wine vinegar	4 heads Belgian endive (about 1 pound), cut in quarters length-wise
	2 tablespoons fresh lemon juice	
1/2 cup chopped onion	1 tablespoon Dijon mustard	
1/4 cup finely chopped carrot	1/2 cup walnut oil	20 scallions, trimmed
	1 tablespoon chopped fresh parsley	1/2 cup vegetable oil
	12 links fresh pork sausage	

Place the lentils in a 3-quart saucepan and add 1½ quarts cold water and 1 teaspoon salt. Bring to a simmer over medium-high heat and then lower the heat to continue to simmer until the lentils are cooked through but not mushy, about 30 to 35 minutes.

While the lentils are cooking, heat 1 tablespoon safflower oil in a medium nonstick sauté pan over medium-high heat. When hot, add the chopped onion, carrot, and celery. Lightly season with salt and pepper and sauté for 8 minutes until tender and flavorful. Transfer the vegetables to a 7-quart nonreactive bowl and set aside until needed.

When the lentils are cooked, drain in a colander. Transfer the lentils to the bowl with the cooked vegetables. In a separate bowl, whisk together the red wine vinegar, lemon juice, and Dijon mustard. Add the remaining 1/2 cup safflower oil and the walnut oil and whisk vigorously to combine. Add the chopped parsley and whisk to combine. Add 1/2 cup of this vinaigrette to the bowl with the lentils and vegetables, and stir to incorporate. Cover the bowl with plastic wrap and set aside at room temperature until needed. Also set aside the remaining 1 cup of vinaigrette at room temperature until needed.

Place the sausage links on a baking sheet with sides. Puncture each sausage several times with a fork. Add 1 cup of water. Place the baking sheet on the grill over medium-high heat. Close the cover and cook for 20 minutes. Remove the

baking sheet with the sausage from the grill and transfer the sausage to a platter lined with paper towels.

Brush the portobello mushroom caps, cut surfaces of the Belgian endive, and the scallions with the vegetable oil and season with salt and pepper. Grill the mushrooms, endive, and scallions over medium-high heat. Grill the mushroom caps for about 8 minutes, turning once; grill the Belgian endive for 5 minutes and the scallions for 2 minutes. Keep warm while grilling the sausage. Grill the sausage over medium-low heat for 5 to 6 minutes, until golden brown and cooked through.

Place about 1 cup of the lentil mixture onto each of 4 plates. Divide and artfully arrange the mushrooms, Belgian endive, and scallions onto each portion of lentils. Dress each portion with 2 to 3 tablespoons remaining vinaigrette. Place 4 sausage links on each plate and serve immediately.

GRILLED SADDLE OF LAMB
WITH COCONUT PEARS

Fritz Sonnenschmidt

Delicious flavors come together in this unique balance of the sweet and the savory.
– Serves 8

3 ½ pounds saddle of lamb, trimmed

5 tablespoons honey

1 teaspoon curry powder

2 tablespoons freshly squeezed lemon juice

2 tablespoons olive oil

4 ripe pears

Vegetable oil

2 tablespoons butter

1 cup grated unsweetened coconut

1 teaspoon sugar

Score the side of the lamb over the rib bones in a diamond shape ½ inch deep. In a small bowl, mix the honey, curry, lemon juice, and olive oil, and brush well over the saddle. Place in a roasting pan and cover. Marinate in the refrigerator for 4 hours.

Preheat grill to medium-high heat (350 degrees F). Place saddle in the center of the grill and cook 25 to 30 minutes; turn often and brush with the marinade.

While the lamb is grilling, peel the pears, cut in half, and remove the cores. Spray with vegetable oil and grill over medium-high heat for 5 minutes.

In a sauté pan, melt the butter. Add the coconut and stir until golden brown. Add sugar and stir till the sugar melts. Toss the pears in this mixture in the pan.

Remove the lamb from grill and allow to rest for 5 to 10 minutes. Slice and serve with the pears, French baguettes, and grilled rosemary tomatoes.

TAGLIATE
WITH ARUGULA AND GRILLED VEGETABLES

Fritz Sonnenschmidt

An old adage claims, "The less you do to a good steak, the better it tastes." How appropriately this is applied in this straightforward recipe by Chef Jon Espelage of Ristorante Tuscany at the World Center Marriott in Orlando. Be sure to use only high-quality olive oil and freshly cracked pepper for maximum flavor. – **Serves 4**

4 (1-inch-thick) New York
   strip steaks
Salt and freshly ground black
   pepper

Extra virgin olive oil
1 large zucchini

2 large beefsteak tomatoes
1 bunch arugula

Rub the steaks with salt, pepper, and olive oil. Grill each steak over medium-high heat for 3 to 4 minutes on each side.

Meanwhile, slice the zucchini and tomatoes 1/2 inch thick. Drizzle with olive oil and season to taste with salt and pepper. Place the vegetables on the grill over indirect heat. Grill the zucchini for about 2 minutes on each side and the tomatoes for just under 1 minute on each side.

In a large bowl, toss the arugula with olive oil, salt, and pepper. Arrange the arugula loosely on a large serving platter and place several slices of grilled zucchini and tomatoes on the side. Slice the steak against the grain and fan over the vegetables. Drizzle the entire plate with a little extra virgin olive oil for extra flavor and serve.

BODACIOUS T-BONE STEAKS
WITH SEXY BARBECUE SAUCE

Fritz Sonnenschmidt

(Reprinted from Weber's Big Book of Grilling, Chronicle Books, 2001)

T-bone steak is well suited for the grill. Trim only the external fat and be sure to use tongs to turn the steak while cooking; a fork may pierce the meat and allow the savory juices to escape. – **Serves 4**

Sexy Barbecue Sauce

$1/2$ cup dry red wine

$1/2$ cup ketchup

$1/4$ cup dark molasses

1 tablespoon Dijon mustard

1 tablespoon Worcestershire sauce

2 tablespoons red wine vinegar

$1/2$ teaspoon chile powder

$1/2$ teaspoon kosher salt

$1/2$ teaspoon celery seeds

$1/4$ teaspoon curry powder

$1/4$ teaspoon ground cumin

T-Bone Steaks

2 T-bone steaks (about 2 pounds and $1 1/2$ inches thick each)

Vegetable oil

Kosher salt and freshly ground black pepper

To make the sauce: In a medium saucepan, combine all the sauce ingredients with $1/2$ cup water. Mix well. Bring to a simmer over medium heat and cook, uncovered, stirring occasionally, until about $2/3$ cup remains, about 30 minutes. Allow to cool to room temperature.

To prepare the steaks: Lightly brush both sides of the steaks with vegetable oil and season generously with salt and pepper. Grill the first side of the steaks directly over high heat for 6 minutes. Turn the steaks over and cook the second side for 5 minutes. Continue to cook the steaks to desired doneness.

Remove the steaks from the grill. Season again with salt and pepper. Let rest for 3 to 5 minutes, during which time the internal temperature will rise about 5 degrees. You can serve the steaks whole or cut the sirloin strips and tenderloins away from the bones and then cut the meat into $1/4$-inch-thick slices. Serve warm with the barbecue sauce.

GRILLED PORK STEAK
WITH WARM POTATO SALAD

Fritz Sonnenschmidt

Today's consumer no longer needs to rely on the butcher to "trim the fat" from their pork. Today's hogs are raised leaner, meeting the demand for quality pork with less fat. Pork steaks are a wonderful cut. – **Serves 4**

Pork Steaks

4 (6 to 8-ounce) pork steaks, cut from the butt

Salt and freshly ground black pepper

1 tablespoon golden mustard

2 tablespoons vegetable oil

Potato Salad

6 ounces bacon, diced

1 red onion, peeled and sliced

2 cloves garlic, peeled and finely chopped

1/4 cup apple cider vinegar

1 tablespoon mustard

1/2 to 1 tablespoon sugar

2 1/2 pounds Yukon Gold potatoes, cooked in their skins

2 tablespoons chopped fresh dill

2 tablespoons fresh parsley

1/2 teaspoon caraway seeds

Olive oil, if needed

Salt and freshly ground black pepper to taste

Boston lettuce leaves

To prepare the pork steaks: Pound pork steaks lightly. Season with salt and pepper. Brush with mustard and oil. Grill over medium-high heat for 3 minutes on each side or to desired doneness.

To make potato salad: Brown the bacon in a skillet until crisp. Remove and drain on paper towels. Add onions to bacon fat and sauté for 2 to 3 minutes. Add garlic and cook for 1 minute.

Deglaze pan with vinegar. Add mustard and sugar. Peel and slice the potatoes, and add them to the pan. Add dill, parsley, and caraway seeds and toss. (If too dry, add some oil.) Season with salt and pepper. Toss and add the bacon.

On individual plates, arrange warm potato salad on a Boston lettuce leaf. Place a pork steak alongside and serve immediately.

GRILLED ANGUS STEAK
WITH ASSORTED GRILLED PEPPERS, GRILLED GARLIC, AND GORGONZOLA

Fritz Sonnenschmidt

When choosing a steak to grill, be sure to find one with good marbling. The finer the marbling, the tenderer the steak. The fat content will cook off while grilling and keep the meat moist and tender. – **Serves 6**

2 red bell peppers

2 yellow bell peppers

2 green bell peppers

1 head garlic

½ cup (1 stick) butter

3 tablespoons finely diced shallots

2 cups red wine

6 Angus steaks (approximately 6 ounces each)

Salt and freshly ground black pepper

Olive oil

6 ounces Gorgonzola, coarsely grated

3 tablespoons chopped chives

10 scallions, trimmed

Grill peppers over medium heat (350 degrees F) until blackened. Place the peppers in a plastic bag and allow to rest for 10 minutes. Peel under running water. Cut the peppers into halves, remove seeds, and cut into strips.

Grill garlic over medium heat for 10 to 15 minutes. Remove from the grill and squeeze out the soft cloves.

In a large skillet, heat 2 tablespoons butter and sauté shallots for 2 minutes. Add the garlic and wine, and reduce to 6 tablespoons. Remove from the heat and place in a bowl.

Season the steaks with salt and pepper. Brush with oil and grill over medium-high heat to desired doneness.

In a skillet, toss the peppers in oil, salt, and pepper to taste, and heat. Sprinkle with Gorgonzola cheese and place on a serving platter. Top with the grilled steaks.

Whip the remaining 6 tablespoons butter into the garlic sauce to create an emulsion. Add chopped chives. Spoon over the steaks. Grill the scallions over medium-high heat for 3 seconds and add to the platter as a garnish. Serve with new potatoes.

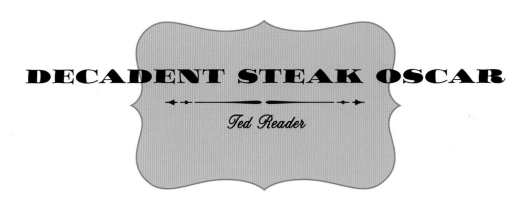

DECADENT STEAK OSCAR

Ted Reader

With the rich flavors of crab and Brie, this recipe makes an elegant version of "surf and turf." Serve this at your next dinner party or divide the recipe in half for a romantic supper for two. – **Serves 4**

1 pound fresh asparagus
4 (12-ounce) New York strip loin
   steaks
¼ cup olive oil
4 cloves garlic, minced
Salt and freshly ground black
   pepper

¼ cup (½ stick) butter
½ cup chopped shallots
1 pound Dungeness crabmeat,
   picked clean of shell
2 tablespoons Dijon mustard
2 teaspoons chopped fresh dill

2 scallions, finely chopped
Cayenne pepper
1 (125-gram) wheel Brie, cut into
   12 wedges

In a large pot over high heat, blanch asparagus in boiling water until tender-crisp. Cool under cold running water; drain and set aside.

Brush the steaks with olive oil and sprinkle with minced garlic, salt, and pepper, pressing the seasoning into the meat. Set aside.

Preheat grill to medium-high.

Melt the butter in a large frying pan over medium-high heat. Sauté the shallots for 2 to 3 minutes, or until transparent and tender. Remove from heat and add the crabmeat, mustard, dill, and scallions and season to taste with cayenne, black pepper, and salt.

Grill the steaks for 3 to 4 minutes per side for medium rare. Divide the crab mixture into 4 equal portions and spread 1 portion evenly on top of each steak. Top each steak with 3 slices of Brie and 3 asparagus spears. Close the lid and cook for 1 to 2 minutes or until the cheese starts to melt.

Serve immediately with grilled potato rounds.

BETTER BUTTER BURGER

Ted Reader

(Reprinted from Sticky Fingers and Tenderloins, Prentice-Hall Canada, 2001)

For the ultimate juicy burger, indulge yourself with 80% to 85% lean ground beef. Much of the fat will cook off during the grilling process but will keep the burger extremely moist. – **Serves 4**

2 pounds regular ground beef
1 cup diced ham
3 tablespoons butter, softened
1 onion, finely chopped
4 to 5 cloves garlic, minced

1 tablespoon chopped fresh
   parsley
1 tablespoon Worcestershire sauce
2 tablespoons coarse-grain
   mustard
1 tablespoon Bone Dust Barbecue
   Spice (see page 29)

1 tablespoon salt
2 tablespoons freshly ground
   black pepper
4 burger buns

Preheat the grill to medium-high heat.

In a large bowl, mix together the beef, ham, butter, onion, garlic, parsley, Worcestershire sauce, mustard, barbecue spice, salt, and black pepper. Form the mixture into four 8-ounce patties as uniform in size as possible. A flatter burger will cook more evenly and faster than a ball-shaped burger.

Grill burgers for 8 to 10 minutes per side for medium well. Lightly toast burger buns, cut side down, until crisp and golden brown.

Serve with your favorite burger garnishes. I like the works, and my list of the works is obscene.

THE ULTIMATE BURGER GARNISH LIST

Ketchup
Mustard
  prepared, Dijon, Pommery,
  honey mustard, or spicy
Relish
  green, zucchini, tomato,
  or corn
Pickles
  sour dills, bread and butter,
  or kosher
Onions
  red, white, yellow, sweet or
  tart; raw, fried, or grilled
Salsa
  mild, medium, or hot
Guacamole
Cheese
  aged Cheddar, Swiss, Brie,
  Cambazola, mozzarella, blue
  cheese, jalapeño Jack or
  Muenster

Back bacon
Bacon
Italian sausage patty
Bratwurst sausage
Fried egg
Grilled portobello mushrooms
Lettuce
  greenleaf, redleaf, iceberg,
  or romaine
Tomato
  red, yellow, or green as
  long as they are fresh and
  full of flavor
Grilled vegetables
  peppers, mushrooms, onions
Barbecue sauce

GRILL WOK FLANK STEAK FAJITAS

Ted Reader

The latest outdoor culinary rage? Wok cooking on the grill. Weber's new line of wok pans are fitted for the kettle grills and produce phenomenal results. The high, even temperature of the coals heat the pan up quickly and create the perfect stir-fry environment. – **Serves 4**

1 1/2 pounds beef flank steak
1 (12-ounce) can beer
2 tablespoons chopped chipotle pepper
1 tablespoon chopped fresh chives
1 tablespoon chopped fresh parsley
2 tablespoons extra virgin olive oil
2 tablespoons malt vinegar

2 tablespoons Bone Dust Barbecue Spice (see page 29) plus extra to taste
1 tablespoon vegetable oil
2 leeks, sliced diagonally
1 green pepper, sliced
1 red pepper, sliced
1 yellow pepper, sliced
1 large onion, sliced
2 portobello mushrooms, sliced

Salt and freshly ground black pepper
1/2 cup barbecue sauce
2 tablespoons hot sauce
8 (7-inch) flour tortillas
1 cup sour cream
1 cup guacamole
1 cup salsa
1 cup grated Cheddar cheese

Using a sharp knife, trim the flank steak of excess fat and sinew. Place the steak in a baking pan and pour half the beer, the chipotle pepper, chives, parsley, olive oil, malt vinegar, and 2 tablespoons barbecue spice over the meat. Cover and refrigerate, allowing the steak to marinate for 4 to 6 hours.

Preheat grill to high and place wok attachment over coals.

Remove steak from marinade (discarding marinade) and thinly slice the steak on the bias and set aside.

Add vegetable oil to the wok. Add the leeks, peppers, onion and mushroom to the wok and stir to prevent burning, for 5 to 8 minutes or until vegetables are cooked. Season with salt, pepper, and barbecue spice. Push the vegetables to the side of the wok and add the beef. Stir-fry for 2 to 3 minutes, until the beef is cooked rare to medium rare. Add the remaining beer, the barbecue sauce, and hot sauce and stir well for 2 minutes to incorporate.

Place everything from the wok into a large serving bowl and serve with warmed flour tortillas, sour cream, guacamole, salsa, and grated Cheddar cheese.

APPLE GINGER PORK CHOPS
WITH GRILLED APPLE RINGS AND CORN BREAD

Fritz Sonnenschmidt

Any firm fleshed fruit on the grill is undeniably delectable. The grilling process draws out the natural fruit sugars, and when fruit is paired with pork, it is a hands-down winning combination. – **Serves 4**

Pork Chops

3/4 cup apple juice

Salt and freshly ground black pepper

1 teaspoon grated or shaved fresh ginger

1 clove garlic, finely minced

2 tablespoons olive oil

4 (6-ounce) center-cut pork chops

Vegetable oil

Apple Rings

4 Golden Delicious apples

Vegetable oil

Corn Bread

1 cup cornmeal

3/4 cup bread flour

1 1/2 teaspoons baking powder

1/2 cup sugar

1 teaspoon salt

2 eggs

1/2 cup buttermilk

1/4 cup vegetable oil

Freshly cracked black pepper

To prepare the pork chops: In a small bowl, combine the apple juice, salt and pepper to taste, ginger, garlic, and oil. Mix well and pour over the chops in a baking pan. Cover and marinate in the refrigerator for 2 hours. Remove the chops from the marinade and pat dry with paper towels. Brush the chops with oil and grill over medium-high heat until slightly brown or medium well (pink), approximately 8 minutes on each side, or to your preference. In a small saucepan over medium-high heat, reduce the marinade to a syrupy consistency and brush on the chops.

To make apple rings: Remove the cores from the apples but do not peel. Cut the apples into 1- to 2-inch-thick slices. Brush with marinade and oil. Grill over medium-high heat for 1 minute on each side.

To make the corn bread: Preheat the grill to medium heat (350 degrees F). Lightly oil a 9-inch square baking pan. In a large bowl, combine the cornmeal, flour, baking powder, sugar, and salt in a mixing bowl. In another bowl, mix together the eggs, buttermilk, and oil until smooth and well blended. Add wet ingredients to dry and mix well. Pour batter into prepared pan and place on grill for approximately 25 to 30 minutes. Check for doneness by inserting a toothpick in the center. If the toothpick comes out clean, remove the pan from the heat, cool, and cut into portions.

Place apple rings on a large serving platter. Arrange pork chops on the side and drizzle the remaining marinade over the apples. Serve with buttered corn bread sprinkled with crushed pepper.

GRILLED VEAL CHOPS
WITH MUSHROOM FRICASSEE AND BUFFALO MOZZARELLA

Ted Reader

Because veal is a delicately flavored meat, it is a good idea to prepare it with a robust sauce or rub. In this particular recipe, the veal is served with a hearty mushroom fricassee, creating a terrific balance of flavors. – **Serves 4**

4 (6-ounce) bone-in veal rack chops
6 to 8 cloves garlic, chopped, plus
    4 cloves minced
Salt and freshly cracked black
    pepper
1 cup maple syrup
1 cup barbecue sauce

¼ cup cognac
¼ cup olive oil
4 shallots, finely chopped
2 cups sliced oyster mushrooms
1 cup sliced shiitake mushrooms
1 cup sliced button mushrooms
1 cup sliced chanterelle mushrooms

1 cup sliced portobello mushrooms
1 tablespoon chopped fresh parsley
½ cup demiglace (reduced veal
    stock)
¼ cup white wine
2 large balls buffalo mozzarella
    cheese, each sliced into 4 pieces

Season the chops with the chopped garlic, salt, and cracked black pepper. Preheat the grill to medium-high heat.

In a small bowl, combine the maple syrup, barbecue sauce, and cognac. Set this basting sauce aside until you are ready to grill.

Heat the oil in a large pot over medium-high heat. Sauté shallots, minced garlic, and all of the mushrooms for 8 to 10 minutes, stirring occasionally, until all the mushrooms are tender. Add the demiglace and wine. Bring mixture to a boil, reduce heat to low and let simmer, stirring occasionally for 10 minutes. Season with salt and pepper. Set aside to keep warm.

Grill the veal chops for 6 to 8 minutes per side, brushing each chop with the basting sauce, for medium-rare doneness.

When the chops are just done, set them to the side of the grill. Top each chop with 2 or 3 slices of mozzarella cheese. Close grill lid and allow the cheese to melt and bubble.

Remove from grill and serve with mushroom fricassee.

PULLED PORK SUNDAES

Ted Reader

These sundaes are not of the traditional summer variety. Instead of ice cream, the components are made from the perfect backyard barbecue: pork, beans, and coleslaw. This treat will make a memorable impression and find its way into your summer bill of fare. – **Serves 10 to 12**

Pulled Pork

1 (7- to 9-pound) bone-in Boston butt pork

1 cup Bone Dust Barbecue Spice (see page 29)

Mesquite or hickory smoking chunks, soaked in water for at least 30 minutes

2 cups Jack Daniel's sour mash whiskey plus extra if needed

3 cups hickory smoke–flavored barbecue sauce

½ cup malt vinegar

¼ cup brown sugar

Salt and freshly ground black pepper

Coleslaw

½ small white cabbage, thinly sliced

½ small red cabbage, thinly sliced

1 onion, thinly sliced

2 large carrots, grated

1 tablespoon cider vinegar

Salt and freshly ground black pepper

Bone Dust Barbecue Spice to taste

½ cup vegetable oil

2 tablespoons chopped fresh parsley

1 large can baked beans

12 wedges garlic toast (optional)

Rub pork with the barbecue spice, pressing it into the meat. Prepare your smoker according to manufacturer's instructions to 225 degrees F. Place pork shoulder on the top rack of smoker and close the lid. Add soaked wood chunks to the charcoal for the first 2 hours of cooking.

Smoke pork for 6 to 8 hours, until a meat thermometer inserted in the thickest part of the meat nearest the bone reads 180 degrees F. (Also, when you pull on the blade bone, it will pull clean from the meat.) During cooking, adjust the air vents to maintain a temperature of

225 degrees F and replenish coals and water as needed. If the meat looks dry, spray with a little water or whiskey.

Transfer pork to a bowl and loosely cover with plastic wrap. Refrigerate for at least 24 hours or up to a week.

Put pork in a large pot. Add 1 cup of the whiskey and enough water to cover. Bring to a boil, reduce to low, and simmer for 2 hours.

Meanwhile, prepare the sauce. In a medium bowl, whisk together the remaining 1 cup whiskey, barbecue sauce, vinegar, and brown

sugar. Set aside until needed.

Remove pork from the pot and let rest for 10 minutes. With a fork or your hands, shred meat from the bone into small strips. Place meat into a large bowl and add sauce a little at a time, mixing thoroughly.

In a large bowl, combine all ingredients for the coleslaw. Set aside.

In a medium saucepan, gently heat the baked beans and you are ready to assemble.

Fill a third of a large mason jar with baked beans. Next, gently layer the shredded pork and pack down, so that the mason jar is two-thirds full. Top with a generous serving of coleslaw, and garnish with a wedge of toasted garlic bread, if desired.

THICK-CUT BONE-IN SOUTHWEST PORK CHOP
WITH CHIPOTLE AND CORN STUFFING

Ted Reader

Pork chops that are at least an inch thick have a better chance of being tender and juicy—anything thinner tends to dry out. For the juiciest results, select chops that are pink in color. – **Serves 4**

2 ears corn, soaked in water in their husks

1 small red onion, peeled and sliced 1/2 inch thick

4 roasted red peppers

4 slices double-smoked bacon, chopped

2 cups grated manchego cheese, or 3 cups diced

2 chipotle peppers, chopped

2 to 3 cloves garlic, chopped

1/4 cup coarse-grain mustard

2 tablespoons chopped cilantro

Salt, freshly ground black pepper, and Bone Dust Barbecue Spice (see page 29)

1 cup gourmet barbecue sauce

1/4 cup white wine

2 tablespoons honey

1 tablespoon hot sauce

1 teaspoon Worcestershire sauce

4 (1-pound) thick-cut pork loin chops, about 2 inches thick, bone in and frenched

1/4 cup olive oil

Prepare the stuffing by grilling the corn and red onion slices over medium heat for 5 to 10 minutes until lightly charred. Cut kernels from cob and chop the red onion. Combine corn and onion in a bowl with the red pepper, bacon, cheese, chipotle peppers, garlic, mustard, and cilantro. Season to taste with salt, pepper, and Barbecue Spice. Set aside.

In a small bowl, combine the gourmet barbecue sauce, white wine, honey, hot sauce, and Worcestershire sauce. Season to taste with salt, pepper, and barbecue spice. Set aside for basting.

Preheat the grill to medium-high heat.

Place the chops on a flat work surface. With a boning knife, make an incision along the fleshy side of each chop about 2 inches long. Cutting in a semicircular motion with the tip of the knife, create a pocket on the inside of the chop. Use your fingers to open the pocket up and carefully but firmly fill the pocket with the stuffing. Rub the pork chops with the olive oil, salt, pepper, and barbecue spice, pressing the spices into the meat. Wrap the bones in foil to prevent burning.

Place the chops on the grill and grill indirectly for 25 to 30 minutes, until just cooked through and the juices run clear. Baste with your barbecue sauce during the last 15 minutes and before serving.

STUFFED PORK BABY BACK RIBS
WITH CURRIED FRUIT COMPOTE

Ted Reader

(Reprinted from Hot and Sticky BBQ, Alpha Books, 2003)

Baby back ribs are cut from the loin. They are leaner and thinner than spareribs and country-style ribs. Pork ribs have been backyard fare since barbecue was invented, most likely from the West Indies and drawing on African roots. This recipe, with its extra stuffing, will impress any outdoor chef. – **Serves 4**

Stuffed Pork Ribs

2 (2- to 3-pound) racks pork spareribs

2 tablespoons Bone Dust Barbecue Spice (see page 29)

1 lemon, thinly sliced

2 cups apple juice

1 loaf (about 22 slices) enriched white bread

2 cloves garlic, minced

1 onion, diced

2 stalks celery, diced

6 slices bacon, fully cooked and chopped

1 cup diced dried apricots

1/2 cup golden raisins

1 tablespoon chopped fresh rosemary

1/2 cup boiling water

1/4 cup (1/2 stick) melted butter

Salt and freshly ground black pepper to taste

Vegetable oil

Curried Fruit Compote

1 cup diced fresh pineapple

1/2 cup diced dried apricots

1/2 cup candied cherries, halved

1/4 cup candied orange peel

1/4 cup golden raisins

1/2 cup corn syrup

1/4 cup plum sauce

1 tablespoon minced fresh ginger

1 tablespoon curry paste

Salt to taste

To prepare the ribs: Preheat the oven to 325 degrees F.

With a sharp knife, score the membrane on the backside of the ribs in a diamond pattern. Rub with the barbecue spice, pressing the seasoning into the meat. Lay ribs, meat side down, in a roasting pan. Lay 3 or 4 lemon slices on the back of each rib and pour in the apple juice. Cover tightly with a lid or aluminum foil.

Braise the ribs until tender, 2 to 2 1/2 hours. Let cool slightly. Reduce the oven temperature to 200 degrees F.

While the ribs are cooling, prepare the stuffing. Cut the bread into 1/2-inch cubes. Spread on a baking sheet and heat in the oven until dry, about 30 minutes.

In a large bowl, combine the dried bread, garlic, onion, celery, bacon, apricots, raisins, and rosemary. Add the boiling water and melted butter, stirring to mix fully. Season with salt and pepper. The stuffing should hold together but still be moist.

Lay a pork rib, curved side up, on a work surface. Stuff the curved side with all the stuff-

ing, pressing it firmly to form a log along the inside of the rib. Place another rib, curved side down, on top of the stuffing, pressing firmly so it adheres. Tie the ribs together with kitchen string at 2-inch intervals. Brush the ribs with vegetable oil.

Grill the ribs indirectly over medium heat, with the grill lid closed, until lightly charred and the stuffing is hot, 10 to 15 minutes per side. (Indirect heat will enable you to use your grill more like an oven and grill-roast the ribs.) Remove the ribs from the grill and let stand for 5 minutes.

To make the fruit compote: In a medium saucepan, combine the pineapple, apricots, cherries, orange peel, raisins, corn syrup, plum sauce, ginger, and curry paste with 1/4 cup water. Bring to a boil over medium-high heat, stirring. Reduce the heat to medium-low and simmer for 15 minutes. Season with salt. Let cool. (Makes about 3 1/4 cups.)

Cut between every second bone of the ribs and place them on a large serving platter. Serve immediately with the cooled fruit compote.

SEAFOOD

Chapter 4

GRILLED MAHI MAHI AND SAUTÉED BACKFIN CRABMEAT
WITH ZUCCHINI, SPINACH, AND CREAM

Marcel Desaulniers

Mahi mahi is an excellent food fish, and the large flaked, sweetly moist meat has exquisite flavor. The skin can be left intact to prevent the delicate texture of the meat from falling through the grill. – **Serves 4**

2 tablespoons fresh lemon juice
2 tablespoons extra virgin olive oil
1 tablespoon chopped fresh dill
Salt and freshly ground black pepper

4 (4- to 5-ounce) skinless mahi mahi fillets
1 cup heavy cream
2 pounds zucchini, washed and lightly peeled
1/4 cup (1/2 stick) butter, softened

1/2 pound flat-leaf spinach, stemmed, washed, and dried, and cut widthwise into 1/2-inch-wide strips
1 pound lump backfin crabmeat, well picked of shell

In a 3-quart nonreactive bowl, whisk together the lemon juice, olive oil, and chopped dill. Add salt and pepper to taste and whisk to combine. Add the mahi mahi fillets and turn each a few times to coat with the marinade. Wrap each portion individually in plastic wrap and refrigerate until ready to grill.

Heat the cream in a 3-quart saucepan over medium heat. Season lightly with salt. When the cream begins to simmer, lower the heat so the cream will simmer slowly, but not boil. Place a stainless steel ladle in the saucepan with the cream and occasionally stir the cream to keep it from foaming out of the saucepan. Simmer the cream until it has reduced by half, about 30 minutes. Strain the reduced cream and hold warm in a double boiler.

While the cream is heating, cut the zucchini into long ovals about 1/4 inch thick. Brush with olive oil, season with salt and pepper and grill over medium-high heat.

Grill the mahi mahi fillets over medium-high heat until done, about 4 1/2 minutes on each side. Keep the fish warm while finishing the recipe.

Melt the butter in a large nonstick sauté pan over medium heat. When hot, add the spinach. Season with salt and pepper and sauté until hot, about 5 minutes. Add the crabmeat and stir to incorporate. Heat for another 2 minutes, until the crab is hot.

Arrange the grilled zucchini on warm plates. Top with the hot crab and spinach mixture. Place a grilled mahi mahi fillet on top of this and drizzle some hot cream over all. Serve immediately.

GRILLED SHRIMP
WITH AVOCADO SWEET CORN RELISH

Fritz Sonnenschmidt

It is not surprising that shrimp is the most popular seafood in the United States. With its distinctive flavor and tender meat, this recipe is both refreshing and delicious. – **Serves 4**

½ cup olive oil

3 tablespoons freshly squeezed lime juice

1 tablespoon honey

2 tablespoons soy sauce

16 large (16–20) fresh shrimp, peeled and deviened

1 ear corn, soaked in water in the husk, grilled, husk removed and kernels cut off

½ red onion, sliced and grilled, then chopped

2 tablespoons chopped cilantro plus a cilantro sprig (for garnish)

1 clove garlic, grilled and mashed

1 avocado, cubed

Salt and freshly ground black pepper to taste

In a small stainless steel bowl, combine ¼ cup olive oil, 1 tablespoon lime juice, the honey, and 1 tablespoon soy sauce. Add the shrimp, toss to coat, cover, and marinate in the refrigerator for 30 minutes.

In a medium bowl, combine the grilled corn kernels, grilled red onions, the remaining 2 tablespoons lime juice, remaining ¼ cup olive oil, remaining 1 tablespoon soy sauce, cilantro, and the mashed grilled garlic. Fold in the avocado and mix gently. Season with salt and pepper. Cover and set aside.

Remove the shrimp from marinade and grill over medium heat for 2 minutes on each side.

Arrange the relish on a serving platter. Top with grilled shrimp and garnish with a sprig of cilantro. Serve immediately.

GRILLED SEA SCALLOPS
WITH BLACK-EYED PEAS, CABBAGE, TOMATOES, AND SLAB BACON

Marcel Desaulniers

Be selective when purchasing scallops. They should be firm and range in color from pale beige to creamy pink. If scallops are stark white, it's a sign that they've been soaked in water—a method to increase their weight. – **Serves 4**

- 1/2 cup dried black-eyed peas, washed, picked over, and soaked for 12 hours
- 2 teaspoons salt
- 1/2 pound hickory-smoked slab bacon
- 3 tablespoons peanut oil
- 1 pound green cabbage (discolored and tough outer leaves removed), cored, quartered, and sliced 1/4 inch thick
- Salt and freshly ground black pepper
- 2 tomatoes, peeled, seeded, and chopped
- 1 1/2 pounds sea scallops, side muscle removed
- 2 whole lemons, cut in half (for garnish)
- 1 bunch watercress, stems trimmed, washed, and dried (for garnish)

Drain the soaked black-eyed peas in a colander. Rinse with cold water and drain thoroughly. Bring 1 quart cold water and 2 teaspoons salt to a boil in a 3-quart saucepan over high heat. Add the black-eyed peas. Adjust the heat and simmer the peas about 40 minutes, until tender but slightly firm to the bite. Drain the cooked peas in a colander and set aside at room temperature until needed.

Preheat the oven to 325 degrees F. Trim the rind and excess fat from the bacon. Cut the bacon into 3/8-inch cubes. Place on a baking sheet and bake for 30 minutes. Transfer the cooked bacon to paper towels to drain. Keep the bacon at room temperature until needed.

In a large nonstick sauté pan, heat 1 tablespoon peanut oil over medium-high heat. When hot, add the diced bacon and sauté for 30 seconds. Add the cabbage, season to taste with salt and pepper, and heat for 2 minutes. Add 2 tablespoons water, and braise the cabbage and bacon for 3 to 5 minutes. Add the cooked black-eyed peas and the chopped tomatoes, season with salt and pepper, and cook until the mixture is hot, 2 to 3 minutes. Keep warm while preparing the scallops.

Combine the scallops with the remaining 2 tablespoons peanut oil. Season with salt and pepper. Divide the scallops into 4 portions and skewer each portion.

Grill the scallop skewers over medium heat for 4 minutes (for tender and delicious scallops, do not overcook). Turn the skewers only once while cooking. Remove from the grill.

Divide the cabbage mixture among 4 warm 9- to 10-inch soup or pasta plates. Remove the grilled scallops from the skewers and place on the cabbage on each plate. Garnish with lemon and watercress. Serve immediately.

GRILLED SALMON
WITH CHILLED PINK GRAPEFRUIT, SPICY BLACK BEANS, AND RICE

Marcel Desaulniers

This unique dish combines as many different textures as it does temperatures. The warm rice gets tossed with room-temperature black beans and plated with salmon hot off the grill. The finishing touch of cool, tart grapefruit ensures an enchanting experience for your taste buds. – **Serves 4**

Spicy Black Beans

1/2 pound dried black turtle beans, picked over, washed, and soaked for 12 hours in 4 cups cold water

1 teaspoon salt plus extra to taste

1 1/2 tablespoons Myer's dark rum

1 1/2 tablespoons raspberry vinegar

1 small yellow onion (about 1/4 pound), cut into 1/4-inch pieces

1 small green pepper (about 1/4 pound), cut into 1/4-inch pieces

1 small red pepper (about 1/4 pound), cut into 1/4-inch pieces

1 clove garlic, minced

1 jalapeño pepper, roasted, skin and seeds removed, and minced

1/2 teaspoon freshly ground black pepper

1 pinch cayenne pepper

2 to 3 dashes Tabasco sauce

Bell Pepper Rice

1 tablespoon olive oil

1 small yellow onion (about 1/4 pound), finely chopped, plus 1/4 cup minced yellow onion

1 small green pepper (about 1/4 pound), cut into 1/4-inch pieces

1 small red pepper (about 1/4 pound), cut into 1/4-inch pieces

Salt and freshly ground black pepper

1 cup converted rice

1 3/4 cups vegetable stock

2 bay leaves

Grilled Salmon

4 (6- to 7-ounce) salmon fillets

2 tablespoons extra virgin olive oil

Salt and freshly ground black pepper

4 whole fresh pink grapefruit (about 3 pounds), peeled and sectioned (for garnish)

To make the black beans: Drain the soaked beans in a colander. Rinse the beans with cold running water, and drain thoroughly. Place the beans in an extra-large saucepan and cover with 4 cups fresh cold water. Add 1 teaspoon salt and stir to combine. Bring the beans to a boil over medium-high heat. Lower the heat and simmer the beans until tender, about 1 hour. Drain the beans in a colander, and transfer them to a large dinner plate. Refrigerate the beans until needed.

Return the saucepan to the heat. Heat the rum, raspberry vinegar, onion, and green and red peppers over medium-high heat. Season with salt. Bring to a simmer and cook for 4 minutes. Add the garlic and jalapeño and stir to combine. Cook for 1 minute.

Return the beans to the saucepan and stir to combine. Add the black pepper, cayenne pepper, and Tabasco sauce. Stir to combine and cook, stirring occasionally, over medium heat for 5 minutes. Reduce the heat to low and cook, stirring occasionally, while preparing the rice.

To make the rice: Preheat the oven to 350 degrees F. Heat the olive oil in a medium ovenproof saucepan over medium heat. When hot, add the chopped onion and peppers. Season with salt and pepper. Cook for 1 minute. Add the rice and stir to coat with the oil and onions. Add the vegetable stock and stir to combine. Add the bay leaves. Bring to a boil over medium-high heat. Cover the pan with a tight-fitting lid or aluminum foil. Place the pan in the preheated oven and bake for 20 minutes undisturbed. Remove the pan from the oven. Remove the 2 bay leaves and discard. Gently stir the rice with a fork. Adjust the seasoning with salt and pepper. Set the covered pan of rice aside to stay warm while grilling the salmon.

To prepare the salmon: Lightly brush the salmon fillets with the olive oil. Season with salt and pepper. Grill the salmon over medium-high heat for about 3 minutes on each side. Turn the salmon fillets only once while cooking. Remove from the grill.

To assemble: Evenly divide the rice among 4 warm plates, forming the rice into a ring about 2 inches wide. Place black beans in the center of each plate, spreading the black beans to fill the inside of the rice rings. Arrange the grapefruit sections in a ring, with the natural curve of the fruit facing the outside of the plate, on top of and between the rice ring and the beans. Place a salmon fillet on top of the beans. Serve immediately.

GRILLED SALMON
WITH LAVENDER BUTTER AND GRILLED MANGOS

Fritz Sonnenschmidt

Lavender has been a favorite herb for centuries. Though commonly known for its uses in perfumes and oils, it is also an incredibly versatile herb for cooking. In the same family as rosemary, it can be used similarly to accent and enhance flavors in many sweet or savory dishes. – **Serves 4**

1 cup (2 sticks) butter, cut into cubes

1/3 cup minced shallots

1/2 cup chardonnay or other dry wine

1/2 cup freshly squeezed lemon juice

1/4 cup loose tea plus extra for the salmon coating

1 tablespoon dried lavender

Salt and freshly ground black pepper to taste

4 (6-ounce) skinless salmon fillets

Olive oil

4 mangos

Fresh lavender flowers (optional, for garnish)

In a small saucepan, heat a few cubes of butter, and sauté shallots for 1 to 2 minutes. Add the wine, lemon juice, tea, and 1 1/2 teaspoons lavender. Bring to a boil and reduce by half. Remove the saucepan from heat and slowly add in the remaining butter cubes, stirring to melt the butter. Strain the sauce through a coffee filter. Add the remaining 1 1/2 teaspoons dried lavender, salt, and pepper. Keep warm.

Season salmon with salt, pepper, and some tea leaves. Spray with oil and grill over medium-high heat, 3 minutes on each side.

Cut the mangos in half and carve out the pits. Cut the fruit in half again and remove the peel. Season with black pepper, spray with oil, and place on the grill to warm.

Place some lavender butter sauce on each of 4 plates. Place the grilled salmon in the center. Garnish with mango and decorate with lavender flowers.

GRILLED MACKEREL
WITH BLACK AND GREEN BEANS, TOMATOES, AND ANCHOVY PESTO

Marcel Desaulniers

Mackerel, also called kingfish, can be cooked in almost any manner, including broiling, baking, and sautéing. It also lends itself well to grilling, as this recipe demonstrates. Its naturally high-fat content keeps this savory fish moist and juicy during the cooking process. – **Serves 4**

½ cup dried black turtle beans, washed, picked over, and soaked for 12 hours in 2 cups cold water

2 tablespoons fresh lemon juice

2 tablespoons safflower oil

1 tablespoon chopped fresh marjoram

Salt and freshly ground black pepper

4 (8-ounce) mackerel fillets

1 pound green beans, trimmed

1 cup loosely packed basil leaves, washed and dried

¼ ounce freshly grated Parmesan cheese

1 tablespoon toasted pine nuts

½ teaspoon minced garlic

2 anchovy fillets

1 tablespoon extra virgin olive oil

4 tomatoes, peeled, seeded, and chopped

2 tablespoons vegetable oil

Drain the soaked beans in a colander. Rinse the beans with cold running water and drain thoroughly before cooking.

Bring 1 quart of lightly salted water to a boil in a 3-quart saucepan over high heat. Add the beans. Adjust the heat and simmer the beans until tender, about 50 minutes. Drain the beans, and then cool to room temperature. Refrigerate until needed.

In a 3-quart nonreactive bowl, whisk together the lemon juice, safflower oil, and marjoram. Season with salt and pepper and whisk to combine. Add the mackerel fillets and turn each a few times to coat with the marinade. Wrap each fillet individually in plastic wrap and refrigerate until ready to grill.

Heat 3 quarts salted water in a 5-quart saucepan over medium-high heat. When the water boils, add the green beans and cook until tender, about 4 to 6 minutes, depending on the thickness of the beans. Drain the beans in a colander and then immediately plunge them into ice water to stop the cooking and keep the beans bright green. Remove them from the water and drain thoroughly. Cover with plastic wrap and refrigerate until needed.

Process the basil leaves in a food processor fitted with a metal blade. Pulse for 15 seconds until the leaves are finely chopped. Scrape down the sides of the bowl with a rubber spatula. Add the Parmesan, pine nuts, garlic, and anchovy fillets and pulse for 5 seconds. Add the olive oil

and pulse until well combined but still coarse in texture, about 10 to 15 seconds. Remove the pesto from the bowl with a rubber spatula, place in a tightly covered container, and refrigerate until needed.

Grill the mackerel fillets, skin side down, over high heat for about 4½ minutes, turn, and grill for another 4 minutes or so on the flesh side. Keep the fish warm while finishing the recipe.

Heat the tomatoes, pesto, and black beans in a large sauté pan over medium-high heat for 5 to 6 minutes, until very hot. Season with salt and pepper.

In a separate large sauté pan, heat the vegetable oil. Add the green beans and cook until hot, about 4 to 5 minutes. Season with salt and pepper.

Evenly divide the tomato, pesto, and black bean mixture and place in a ring around the outside edges of 4 warm plates. Place an equal amount of green beans in the center of each ring. Place a grilled mackerel fillet, skin side up, on the green beans in the center of each plate and serve immediately.

BACON-WRAPPED TROUT
WITH ROSEMARY AND WARM SMASHED POTATOES
DEBBIE-STYLE

Fritz Sonnenschmidt

Bacon wrapping has become a popular method for not only creating a stunning presentation, but also infusing a delicious smokiness to the tender, flaky trout. – **Serves 4**

Smashed Potatoes Debbie-Style

2½ pounds Yukon Gold potatoes

1 tablespoon whole-grain or coarse-grain mustard

1 tablespoon white wine vinegar

2 teaspoons finely chopped capers

Salt to taste

½ teaspoon freshly ground black pepper

3 tablespoons finely chopped shallot

½ cup extra virgin olive oil

⅓ cup chopped fresh flat-leaf parsley

Bacon-Wrapped Trout

4 (10- to 12-ounce) whole trout, or filleted and cleaned

Salt and freshly ground black pepper

8 (4- to 5-inch) fresh rosemary sprigs

12 slices bacon

12 (⅛-inch-thick) lemon slices (for garnish)

To prepare the potatoes: Peel and quarter the potatoes and place them in a 5-quart pot with enough cold salted water to cover them by 2 inches. Place the pot over medium-high heat and simmer, covered, until just tender, 20 to 25 minutes.

While the potatoes are cooking, in a small bowl whisk together the mustard, vinegar, capers, salt, pepper, and shallots. Add the olive oil in a slow steady stream, whisking until the dressing is emulsified.

Drain the potatoes in a colander and cool slightly. With a fork or potato masher, break up the warm potatoes into smaller chunks and stir in the vinaigrette and parsley. Keep the potatoes warm while grilling the fish.

To prepare the trout: Preheat a grill to medium-high.

Place fish on a baking sheet and pat dry. Season the cavity of each trout with salt and pepper. Place 2 rosemary sprigs inside each cavity. Season the outside of the fish with salt and pepper, and then wrap 3 bacon slices around each fish.

Grill fish until the skin and the bacon are crisp, about 8 minutes. Turn fish over gently with a spatula and grill 2 minutes more or until bacon is crisp. Remove the fish from the grill and place on a platter. Decorate with lemon slices. Serve immediately with the warm smashed potatoes.

GRILLED MONKFISH
WITH A PAN ROAST OF OYSTERS, WILD MUSHROOMS, SPINACH, AND LEEKS

Marcel Desaulniers

Monkfish is also called "allmouth," since the fish is mostly head and the head is mostly mouth. In essence, the only edible part of the fish is the tail. When cooked, monkfish is deliciously dense, sweet, and very similar to lobster in both flavor and texture. – **Serves 4**

2 tablespoons vegetable oil

1 tablespoon lemon juice

1/2 teaspoon chopped fresh thyme

1/4 teaspoon finely minced lemon zest

1 1/2 pounds monkfish fillet, cut into 1- to 1 1/2-inch pieces

1 cup heavy cream

Salt and freshly ground black pepper to taste

1 large leek, white part only, split in half, washed, and cut into 2-inch-long thin strips

2 tablespoons butter

1 tablespoon dry white wine

1/4 pound wild mushrooms, stems trimmed or removed as necessary, sliced

2 pints shucked oysters

8 spinach leaves, stemmed, washed, dried, and cut into thin strips

In a 3-quart bowl, whisk together the vegetable oil, lemon juice, chopped thyme, and lemon zest. Add the monkfish pieces and turn them a few times to coat with the marinade. Divide the monkfish into 4 equal portions and skewer. Cover the skewers with plastic wrap and refrigerate them until ready to grill.

Heat the heavy cream in a 3-quart saucepan over medium heat. Lightly season with salt and pepper. Place a ladle in the saucepan and occasionally stir the cream so that it does not foam over the sides. Lower the heat if necessary so that the cream barely simmers. Simmer until it has reduced by half, about 45 minutes. Strain the reduced cream and hold warm in a double boiler.

While the cream is simmering, blanch the leeks in boiling salted water until tender but slightly crunchy, 30 to 40 seconds. Drain the leeks into a strainer and immerse the strainer in ice water. When the leeks are cool, remove them from the ice water, drain them well, and set them aside until needed.

Heat the butter and white wine in a large nonstick sauté pan over medium-high heat. When the mixture comes to a full boil, add the sliced wild mushrooms, season with salt and pepper, and sauté for 4 to 5 minutes.

Add the leeks and oysters, season again with salt and pepper, and heat to a simmer (adjusting the heat as necessary) for 2 to 3 minutes, until the oysters are warm. Add the reduced cream and heat on low while grilling the monkfish skewers.

Season the skewered monkfish with salt and pepper, and then grill them for about 6 minutes over medium heat. Remove the grilled monkfish from the skewers.

Portion the oyster mixture into each of 4 individual warm soup plates. Sprinkle spinach strips over the top, and then place a portion of grilled monkfish on each. Serve immediately.

GRILLED CATFISH FILLET AND ASPARAGUS
WITH POTATOES, CARROTS, AND TURNIPS

Marcel Desaulniers

The abundance of farm-raised catfish in today's markets is a boon to anyone's Southern culinary inclinations. This dish combines the fresh, clean flavor of catfish with the full, rich taste of peanut oil to create a superb, low-fat meal. – **Serves 4**

3 tablespoons peanut oil

1^1/$_2$ tablespoons freshly squeezed lemon juice

Salt and freshly ground black pepper

4 (6- to 8-ounce) catfish fillets

1 pound fresh asparagus

3 russet potatoes, peeled, cut in ^{1}/$_2$-inch cubes, and covered with cold water

1 pound carrots, peeled, cut into ^{1}/$_2$-inch-long pieces, and covered with cold water

^{1}/$_2$ pound white turnips, peeled, cut into ^{1}/$_2$-inch-long pieces, and covered with cold water

^{1}/$_2$ cup extra virgin olive oil

2 tablespoons coarsely chopped fresh French tarragon

2 tablespoons vegetable oil

In a 3-quart noncorrosive bowl, whisk together the peanut oil, lemon juice, and salt and pepper to taste. Add the catfish fillets and turn a few times to coat. Remove the fillets from the marinade. Wrap each fillet individually in plastic wrap and refrigerate for at least 2 hours (and up to 24 hours).

Snap the woody stem from each stalk of asparagus and lightly peel the stalks. Blanch the asparagus in boiling salted water for about 45 seconds, depending on the thickness (the asparagus should remain crisp). Immediately place the asparagus in ice water. When the asparagus is cold, drain thoroughly, cover with plastic wrap, and refrigerate until needed.

Drain and rinse the potatoes, carrots, and turnips under cold running water. Cook in 2 quarts of lightly salted water until tender, about 20 minutes. Drain the cooked vegetables. With a vegetable masher, crush the drained vegetables with the extra virgin olive oil and tarragon. Keep the crushed vegetables warm while grilling the catfish.

Grill the catfish fillets over medium heat for 3 to 3^1/$_2$ minutes on each side. Remove the fillets from the grill and keep warm while grilling the asparagus.

Coat the asparagus stalks with the vegetable oil. Season with salt and pepper. Grill over medium heat for 1^1/$_2$ to 2 minutes, turning as needed to prevent overcharring.

Place an equal amount of crushed vegetables on each of 4 plates. Place a catfish fillet on each portion of crushed vegetables. Place an equal amount of grilled asparagus onto each catfish fillet. Serve immediately.

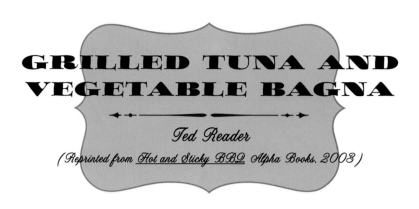

GRILLED TUNA AND VEGETABLE BAGNA

Ted Reader

(Reprinted from Hot and Sticky BBQ, Alpha Books, 2003)

The availability of top-quality "sushi grade" tuna comes no doubt from our infatuation with sushi. If you aren't yet adventuresome enough to try this delicious, meaty fish raw, you should sample it freshly grilled. – **Serves 4**

1 red onion, sliced

1 zucchini, halved and sliced crosswise

1 each red, yellow, and green bell pepper, cut into wedges

8 jumbo white mushrooms, sliced 1/4 inch thick

1 bunch asparagus, trimmed

1/2 cup olive oil plus extra for the tuna

1/2 cup red wine vinegar

Salt and freshly ground black pepper

2 (6-ounce) tuna steaks, about 1 inch thick

3 cloves garlic, minced

4 anchovy fillets, minced

1/4 cup chopped fresh basil

2 tablespoons Dijon mustard

1/2 cup sliced black olives

1/4 cup drained capers

1 (18-inch-long) baguette

2 vine-ripened tomatoes, thinly sliced

2 cups mixed baby greens

Preheat the grill to medium-high heat.

In a large bowl, combine the onion, zucchini, bell peppers, mushrooms, asparagus, 1/4 cup of the olive oil, and 1/4 cup of the vinegar. Toss well. Season to taste with salt and pepper. Place the vegetables in a grill basket and grill until slightly charred and tender, 5 to 6 minutes per side. Transfer the vegetables to a bowl and let cool.

Season tuna steaks with salt, pepper, and a little olive oil. Grill for 2 to 3 minutes per side for medium rare. Let cool.

In a bowl, whisk together the remaining 1/4 cup olive oil and vinegar, the garlic, anchovies, basil, and mustard. Season this dressing to taste with salt and pepper.

Drain the grilled vegetables. Add the olives, capers, and dressing and toss gently.

Cut the baguette in half lengthwise. Arrange the grilled vegetable mixture evenly over the bottom half of the bread. Cut the tuna steaks into 1/2-inch-thick slices. Top the vegetables with layers of tuna, tomatoes, and salad greens. Top with the other half of the baguette. Wrap tightly with plastic wrap and refrigerate for 1 hour to let the flavors blend.

Unwrap the sandwich, and with a sharp serrated knife, slice into 4 or 8 pieces. Serve immediately or wrap the pieces individually for a picnic.

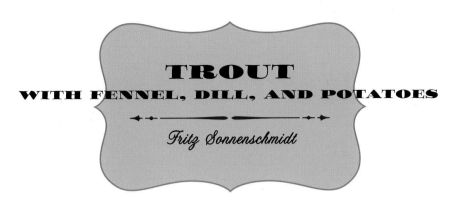

TROUT
WITH FENNEL, DILL, AND POTATOES

Fritz Sonnenschmidt

Dill and fennel share similarities not only in appearance, but in flavor as well. Their assertive aromas pair excellently with oily fish such as trout. Use fresh dill if possible, as the dried version is significantly less flavorful. Unused dill can be stored in the freezer for up to 2 months. – **Serves 2**

2 ounces fennel
2 tablespoons olive oil plus extra
  for spraying
1 tablespoon butter
Salt and freshly ground black
  pepper

2 ounces potatoes
2 (8- to 12-ounce) rainbow trout,
  filleted and trimmed (see note)
4 ounces tomatoes, peeled and
  cut into wedges
1 clove garlic, sliced

1 bay leaf
1 dill sprig
1 sprig fennel leaves

Clean fennel, wash and cut into fine julienne. Reserve the fennel leaves. Heat 2 tablespoons olive oil in a sauté pan. Add 1 teaspoon butter, the fennel, and salt and pepper to taste. Sauté until tender.

Peel potatoes and cut into slices. Spray with oil and grill over medium-high heat for 2 minutes. Spray a sheet of aluminum foil with some oil. Place potato slices on the foil.

Season fish with salt and pepper and place over potatoes. Top with fennel and tomato wedges. Add the garlic, bay leaf, dill, and fennel leaves. Top with the remaining 2 teaspoons butter and close the foil into a pouch. Grill over medium-high heat (350 degrees F) for 15 to 20 minutes.

Remove the pouch from the grill and divide the fillets, potatoes, and vegetables between 2 plates. Serve immediately.

Note: This recipe is also delicious with monkfish, red snapper, or cod.

GRILLED RAINBOW TROUT
WITH A WARM SALAD OF GRILLED SWEET POTATOES, GRAPES, BELGIAN ENDIVE, AND PUMPKIN SEEDS

Marcel Desaulniers

The ever-popular rainbow trout is well suited for the grill. It needs very few seasonings and cooks up in a flash. In this recipe, the fish is served atop a warm potato salad of sorts, drizzled with a surprise finish—a scrumptious pumpkin seed vinaigrette. – **Serves 4**

4 (5- to 6-ounce) rainbow
   trout fillets
¼ cup extra virgin olive oil
Salt and freshly ground
   black pepper
2 tablespoons chopped fresh
   chives
1 cup toasted Chinese pumpkin
   seeds

¼ cup rice wine vinegar
2 tablespoons freshly squeezed
   lemon juice
2 tablespoons creamy peanut
   butter
¼ teaspoon hot sauce
¾ cup peanut oil
3 sweet potatoes
   (about 2 pounds), unpeeled

¼ cup honey
¼ cup vegetable oil
2 tablespoons bourbon
2 heads Belgian endive
½ pound seedless grapes,
   stemmed, washed, and cut in
   half

Brush both sides of the fillets with the extra virgin olive oil. Season well with salt and pepper. Sprinkle with chopped chives. Wrap each fillet individually in plastic wrap and refrigerate until ready to grill.

Place ½ cup toasted pumpkin seeds in the bowl of a food processor fitted with a metal blade. (Save the other ½ cup to garnish the salad.) Process the seeds until powdered.

In a 3-quart nonreactive bowl, whisk together the rice wine vinegar, lemon juice, peanut butter, and hot sauce until smooth. Add the peanut oil in a slow, steady stream while whisking, until incorporated. Add the powdered pumpkin seeds, season with salt as needed, and

whisk to combine. Cover with plastic wrap and set aside at room temperature until needed.

Cook the whole sweet potatoes in a 5-quart saucepan of boiling salted water for 35 minutes. Drain the cooking water from the sweet potatoes. Cool the sweet potatoes under cold running water for 5 minutes. Drain again and refrigerate, uncovered, for 1 hour.

Use a paring knife to peel and trim the ends from the cold sweet potatoes. Slice the sweet potatoes slightly on the bias, into ½-inch-thick slices. (Discard the ends.) Season both sides of the sweet potato slices with salt and pepper. Whisk together the honey, vegetable oil, and bourbon. Dip the sweet potato slices in the honey

mixture, and then grill them over medium heat for 1½ to 2 minutes on each side. Keep the sweet potatoes warm while grilling the trout.

Grill the trout fillets over medium heat, skin side down, for 2 minutes. Transfer the fillets, skin side up, to a baking sheet that has been liberally brushed with olive oil. Place the baking sheet on the grill and close the cover for another 2 minutes.

Cut each endive head in half lengthwise. Cut the core out from each half. Cut each half into ¼-inch-thick slices the length of the endive. Gently wash and dry the endive. Divide and arrange the endive slices onto each of 4 plates. Divide and arrange the grilled sweet potato slices onto the endive. Sprinkle an equal amount of grape halves over each portion. Drizzle 2 to 3 tablespoons of pumpkin dressing over each, and then top with a grilled trout fillet, skin side up. Sprinkle the remaining pumpkin seeds over each salad. Serve immediately.

GRILLED SEA BASS IN ALUMINUM FOIL

Fritz Sonnenschmidt

Pouch cooking is a home chef's dream. Not only is the method convenient, but healthy and flavorful as well. The pouch locks in valuable nutrients and vital moisture, and cleanup is a cinch. – **Serves 4**

1 whole sea bass (about 2 pounds), cleaned and scaled, or 4 fillets (about 1/2 pound each)

1/2 cup dry white wine

1/2 cup finely diced fresh mushrooms

3 tablespoons butter, cut into pieces

2 tablespoons finely chopped shallots

2 cloves garlic, thinly sliced

1 tablespoon finely chopped fresh rosemary

1 bay leaf

1/2 cup diced tomatoes (1/2-inch dice)

Kosher salt

Freshly ground black pepper

Place the sea bass in a foil pan large enough to hold the fish (or 4 fillets) easily. Distribute the wine, mushrooms, butter, shallots, garlic, rosemary, and bay leaf evenly around the fish. Cover lightly with heavy-duty aluminum foil.

Place the pan on the grill over indirect medium heat. Cook until the flesh just begins to flake when tested with a fork, 25 to 30 minutes.

Transfer the sea bass to a serving platter and keep warm. Pour the mixture from the foil pan into a small saucepan. Remove the bay leaf. Add the tomatoes, place over high heat, and simmer for 2 to 3 minutes. Season with salt and pepper to taste. Pour the sauce over the sea bass. Serve immediately.

POACHED SEA BASS
AND VEGETABLES IN GREEN PEPPERCORN CREAM

Fritz Sonnenschmidt

These pouches from your grill will produce delightful aromas of a succulent fish "stew" when opened at the table. Your guests will love it. – **Serves 6**

6 (5-ounce) sea bass fillets

3 tablespoons butter

1 tablespoon minced shallots

1 1/2 cups dry white wine

1 cup dry vermouth

2 bay leaves

1 cup cream

1 tablespoon green peppercorns

Salt to taste

1/2 cup peeled and julienned celery

1/2 cup julienned leeks (white parts only)

1/2 cup julienned fennel

1/2 cup julienned carrots

1 cup peeled, seeded, and julienned tomatoes

2 tablespoons chopped parsley

Cut 6 aluminum foil squares slightly larger than the fish. Cut each fish fillet diagonally into 3 pieces.

Over medium-high heat, melt 1 tablespoon butter in a 2-quart sauté pan. Add shallots, white wine, vermouth, and bay leaves. Reduce this sauce to 1/4-cup syrup consistency. Stir in cream and reduce by a third. Add green peppercorns and salt. Remove bay leaves.

Over high heat, melt the remaining 2 tablespoons butter in a large skillet. Add the celery, leeks, fennel, carrots, 2 tablespoons water, and salt. Cover and cook for 2 minutes and let cool.

Arrange the vegetables on the 6 oiled aluminum squares. Spoon 2 tablespoons of sauce on top of the vegetables, and then add the fish. Spoon the tomatoes over the fish. Pour remaining sauce over fish and close pouch, sealing completely. Grill the pouches over medium heat (375 to 400 degrees F), for approximately 10 to 12 minutes. Remove the pouches with a spatula, place on serving plates, and open the pouches in front of your guests.

TEXAS SURF AND TURF
JUMBO SHRIMP WRAPPED IN BEEF TENDERLOIN

Ted Reader

This version of Surf and Turf is meant as finger food, but the jumbo shrimp wrapped with beef tenderloin is well more than a mouthful. The Asian inspired dipping sauce provides the extra kick that will have your guests begging for more. – **Serves 4**

1/2 cup sweet chili dipping sauce plus extra for dipping

1/4 cup soy sauce

1/4 cup plum sauce

2 scallions, thinly sliced

1 jalapeño pepper, chopped

2 tablespoons chopped cilantro

2 tablespoons minced ginger

2 tablespoons rice vinegar

1 tablespoon mirin

1 teaspoon fish sauce

1 teaspoon sesame oil

Salt and freshly ground black pepper to taste

16 jumbo (under 10 per pound) shrimp, peeled and deveined

16 to 24 slices beef tenderloin, sliced wafer thin (see note)

2 tablespoons olive oil

1 tablespoon Bone Dust Barbecue Spice (see page 29)

In a bowl, whisk together the sweet chili dipping sauce, soy sauce, plum sauce, scallions, jalapeño, cilantro, ginger, rice vinegar, mirin, fish sauce, and sesame oil, and season with salt and pepper. Add the shrimp and marinate for 30 minutes.

Preheat grill to medium-high heat.

Wrap each shrimp around the middle with 1 to 2 pieces of thinly sliced beef tenderloin. Skewer each shrimp onto a wooden chopstick, folding the shrimp and driving the skewer through the tail and the head to stabilize it. Season with olive oil and barbecue spice.

Grill for 3 minutes per side, basting with extra marinade, until the shrimp is just cooked through and opaque in color. Remove from heat and serve with sweet chili dipping sauce.

Note: The beef used here is beef tenderloin that has been frozen and then thinly sliced on a slicing machine and layered. It may be found in specialty Asian food stores frozen. To work with this beef, thaw overnight in the refrigerator and then carefully separate each slice to wrap the shrimp. This beef is used in Vietnamese and Korean barbecues.

BANANA LEAF-WRAPPED GROUPER
WITH JERK BUTTER AND HONEY LEMON SAUCE

Ted Reader

This recipe captures the alluring flavors of the Caribbean with its jerk seasoning: the paste is a combination of garlic, onion, scotch bonnet peppers, thyme, and allspice. Jerk paste can be bought in most grocery stores; however, you may have to visit an Asian market to find banana leaves. You can also substitute heavy-duty aluminum foil if the leaves are hard to locate. – **Serves 4**

4 (6-ounce) grouper fillets
1/4 cup jerk paste
1 cup thinly sliced fresh mango
1/2 Vidalia onion, thinly sliced
1 red pepper, thinly sliced
2 tablespoons chopped cilantro

1/2 cup diced double-smoked bacon
1/4 cup dark rum plus extra for drizzling
Salt, freshly ground black pepper, and Bone Dust Barbecue Spice (see page 29)

4 banana leaves, cut into 1-foot squares
1 pineapple, peeled and cut into 1/2-inch rounds
1/4 cup honey
1 lemon, halved

Season grouper fillets with jerk paste, rubbing the seasoning into the flesh. Set aside for 15 to 20 minutes.

In a bowl, combine the mango, onion, pepper, cilantro, bacon, and rum. Season to taste with salt, pepper, and barbecue spice.

Warm the banana leaf squares over the grill to make them more pliable. Place 1 square on a flat surface. Place a piece of grouper in the center and cover with 1/4 of the marinated tropical fruit and a little of its juice. Fold the sides of the leaf over the fish creating a bundle. Repeat with the other 3 portions. Using butcher twine, secure each bundle.

Preheat grill to medium-high heat.

Place the grouper bundles on the grill and roast for 15 to 20 minutes, turning once. Place the pineapple rounds on the grill and cook for 10 to 12 minutes, turning once, and drizzle with extra rum.

Remove the fish from grill and allow to rest for 2 minutes before opening. Be careful of the escaping steam. Set the fish on a serving platter and drizzle with honey and juice squeezed from the lemon halves. Serve with grilled pineapple.

GRILLED HALIBUT
WITH CUCUMBER HORSERADISH SALAD AND SHRIMP AND AVOCADO BUTTER SAUCE

Ted Reader

(Reprinted from Sticky Fingers and Tenderloins, Prentice-Hall Canada, 2001)

Halibut has a firm steaklike texture, a perfect choice for the grill. The lean, mild-flavored, flaky white flesh absorbs flavors well. Be sure to keep the fish well oiled to prevent sticking and overdrying. – **Serves 6**

Grilled Halibut

1 cup grapefruit juice

¼ cup olive oil

1 small leek, finely diced

2 tablespoons chopped fresh tarragon

1 tablespoon freshly cracked black pepper

Sea salt to taste

6 (10-ounce) halibut T-bone steaks

Avocado Butter Sauce

6 tablespoons cold butter (4 tablespoons cut in pieces)

4 shallots, chopped

2 cloves garlic, chopped

1 small leek, diced

1 jalapeño pepper, finely diced

1 teaspoon finely grated fresh ginger

½ cup grapefruit juice

¼ cup white Riesling

1 cup chopped baby shrimp

1 grapefruit, peeled and segmented

1 avocado, diced

1 tablespoon chopped fresh parsley

Salt and freshly ground black pepper to taste

Cucumber Horseradish Salad

1 English cucumber

1 red onion, thinly sliced

½ cup grated fresh horseradish

2 scallions, chopped

3 tablespoons olive oil

2 tablespoons chopped fresh mint

2 tablespoons freshly squeezed lemon juice

2 tablespoons cider vinegar

1 teaspoon ground cumin

Salt and freshly ground black pepper to taste

To prepare the halibut: In a glass dish large enough to hold the fish, whisk together the grapefruit juice, olive oil, leek, tarragon, black pepper, and salt. Add halibut, turning to coat. Cover and marinate at room temperature for 15 to 30 minutes.

Preheat the grill to medium-high heat. Remove the halibut from the marinade, reserving the marinade for basting. Grill for 5 to 6 minutes per side, basting frequently with the marinade. Remove from the heat and keep warm.

To make the sauce: In a small saucepan over medium-high heat, melt 2 tablespoons of the butter. Sauté the shallots, garlic, leek, jalapeño, and ginger for 3 minutes or until tender. Add the grapefruit juice and wine. Bring to a boil and reduce the liquid by half. Reduce the heat to low and whisk in the remaining butter until smooth. Gently stir in the baby shrimp, grapefruit, avocado, and parsley. Season with salt and pepper. (Makes about 1 cup.)

To make the salad: Cut the cucumber in half lengthwise. Thinly slice the cucumber halves.

In a large bowl, toss together the cucumber, onion, horseradish, scallions, oil, mint, lemon juice, and cumin. Season with salt and pepper. Cover the bowl with plastic wrap and chill.

To serve: On individual plates, place a halibut steak and top with the sauce. Serve the chilled salad alongside.

CEDAR-PLANKED SALMON PINWHEELS

Ted Reader

These flavorful pinwheels make a dramatic presentation when served. Be sure to use the freshest salmon possible, which is easy to recognize. Lightly press the flesh with your finger; if it springs back, it is guaranteed fresh. – **Serves 4**

1 pound crabmeat

¼ cup firm ricotta cheese

1 cup cream cheese

1 pound spinach, blanched and squeezed of excess moisture

2 tablespoons chopped garlic

2 small shallots, chopped

1 teaspoon each chopped fresh thyme, cilantro, dill, and rosemary

2 tablespoons cider vinegar

Salt, freshly ground black pepper, and Bone Dust Barbecue Spice (see page 29)

1 (2- to 3-pound) Atlantic salmon, center cut, boneless, skinless, and butterflied lengthwise

1 (12 by 8 by 1-inch) untreated Western red cedar plank, soaked at least 1 hour

In a large bowl, combine the crabmeat, ricotta cheese, cream cheese, spinach, garlic, shallots, herbs, and cider vinegar. Season to taste with salt, pepper, and barbecue spice.

Place the butterflied salmon on a large sheet of aluminum foil on a flat surface and unfold the salmon. Use your hands to spread the crab and spinach mixture evenly over the salmon to a thickness of ¼ inch, pressing it firmly into the salmon. Starting at the bottom, roll the salmon into a log. Wrap tightly in aluminum foil and refrigerate, to allow the salmon roll to rest and set, for 1 to 2 hours.

Preheat the grill to high heat (450 to 500 degrees F).

Remove the salmon from the refrigerator, and with a sharp knife, cut the salmon roll, with the foil on, into 2-inch pinwheel slices, and transfer them to the presoaked plank.

Place the plank on the grill, close the lid, and grill for 15 to 20 minutes, removing the foil halfway through cooking. Periodically check that the plank is not on fire. If it is, spray the fire with water from a spray bottle to put it out. Remove the plank from the grill and serve the pinwheels on the plank with steamed asparagus.

PROSCIUTTO-WRAPPED SALMON AND SCALLOPS
WITH MAPLE CHILI GLAZE AND RED BEET SALAD

Ted Reader

Sambal is a popular Indonesian condiment made with red chiles. Use sparingly, as even a dollop of this sauce will pack a punch to these prosciutto-wrapped skewers of succulent seafood. – **Serves 4**

Red Beet Salad with Honey Orange Vinaigrette

5 beets, cooked, cooled, and peeled
1 onion, thinly sliced
1 orange, peeled and cut in segments
1 tablespoon chopped fresh thyme
1 teaspoon coarsely ground black pepper
¼ cup orange juice
3 tablespoons olive oil
1 tablespoon orange blossom honey
Salt to taste

Prosciutto-Wrapped Salmon and Scallops

1 tablespoon Bone Dust Barbecue Spice (see page 29)
¼ cup maple syrup
¼ cup orange juice
1 tablespoon chopped fresh thyme
1 tablespoon chopped fresh dill
1 tablespoon sambal chili paste
1 tablespoon olive oil plus extra for drizzling
2 scallions, finely chopped
Salt and freshly ground black pepper to taste
16 fresh jumbo scallops, trimmed of muscle
2 pounds fresh Atlantic salmon, cut into 2-ounce cubes
16 slices prosciutto

To make the salad: Slice the beets in half lengthwise and then thinly slice crosswise. In a medium bowl, thoroughly combine the beets, onion, orange segments, thyme, and pepper.

In a small bowl, whisk together the orange juice, olive oil, and honey. Pour over the beet mixture and mix thoroughly. Season with salt. Chill until ready to serve.

To prepare the salmon and scallops: In a dish large enough to hold all the seafood, whisk together the barbecue spice, maple syrup, orange juice, thyme, dill, sambal, oil, scallions, salt, and pepper.

Drain the scallops well and pat dry with paper towels. Place the scallops and the salmon cubes in the marinade, cover and refrigerate for 15 to 20 minutes.

Remove the fish from the marinade and wrap each cube of salmon and scallop with a half slice of prosciutto. Alternate 4 scallops and 4 salmon cubes each onto 4 skewers. Set aside.

Preheat grill to medium-high heat.

Drizzle the skewers with olive oil and place on the grill. Cook for 3 to 4 minutes per side, or until the bacon is crisp and the scallops are just done. Be careful not to overcook.

Serve immediately with beet salad.

CEDAR-PLANKED SEA BASS
WITH ROASTED RED PEPPER, CRAB AND BACON CRUST

Ted Reader

Planking is a time-tested method of cooking, where foods "bathe" in their own juices. Native Americans of the Pacific Northwest have long used cedar planks to permeate their fish, meats, poultry, and vegetables with its flavorful, woodsy aroma. – **Serves 4**

- 2 tablespoons olive oil
- 1 tablespoon rice vinegar
- 2 to 3 cloves garlic, chopped
- 1 small red onion, diced
- 4 red peppers, peeled, roasted, seeded, and chopped
- 4 slices bacon, cooked crisp and chopped
- ¼ cup grated Parmesan cheese
- 1½ cups lump crabmeat
- Sea salt, freshly ground black pepper, and Bone Dust Barbecue Spice (see page 29)
- 4 (6-ounce) fresh skinless sea bass fillets, about 2 inches thick
- 1 (12 by 8 by 1-inch) untreated Western red cedar plank, soaked at least 1 hour
- 2 fresh limes, cut into wedges (for garnish)

Preheat the grill to high heat (450 to 500 degrees F). In a bowl, combine the olive oil, rice vinegar, garlic, red onion, roasted red peppers, bacon, Parmesan cheese, and crabmeat. Season to taste with salt, pepper, and barbecue spice.

Season sea bass fillets with salt, black pepper, and barbecue spice. Place the sea bass on the presoaked plank and coat the fillets with the red pepper and bacon mixture, using all the mixture. Gently pat it down to adhere.

Place the plank in the grill, close the lid, and grill for 15 to 20 minutes until cooked to medium-well doneness. The fish should flake easily apart.

Periodically check that the plank is not on fire. If it is, spray the fire with water from a spray bottle to put it out.

Carefully remove the planks of sea bass from the grill and allow to rest for 2 minutes. Serve it on the plank with fresh limes.

The *Grilling Maestros* television series was filmed at the Orlando World Center Marriott Resort & Convention Center on their 200 acres of lush tropical grounds.

ACKNOWLEDGMENTS

We applaud our three grilling maestros — Marcel Desaulniers, Ted Reader, and Fritz Sonnenschmidt — whose creative recipes and sparkling television presentations inspire home cooks with many memorable meals along with the skills needed to execute them.

Every maestro, no matter how talented, knows that his or her performance depends on having the highest quality instrument possible. The Weber Stephen Products Co. makes a range of grills that support the artistry of any great griller. Weber introduced the kettle grill in the 1950s, before the concept of grilling was even a blip on most home cooks' radar, and continues as a visionary company whose products have introduced millions of people to the pleasures of outdoor cooking. We are honored to have their support on this project and are especially grateful to Mike Kempster, Sr., for his countless contributions and support. He has been a great guide and inspiration to us in the making of this series.

We are very pleased to have a new sponsor this year — Reynolds — and their latest product, Reynolds Wrap Release Non-Stick Aluminum Foil. Most experienced grillers arm themselves with a roll of aluminum foil at the ready — to cover, protect, wrap, store, and hold their food. A special thank you to Doug Mickle for his tremendous support of the project.

We are also extremely grateful to the Orlando World Center Marriott for their support. Their beautifully landscaped grounds provided the perfect backdrop for this season of *Grilling Maestros.* Their unparalleled hospitality and commitment to customer service ensured a pleasant and efficient production. Special thanks to Michael Quinlan, Tony Alicea, and Will Seton for their assistance.

Thanks to the remarkable generosity of Cuisinart for providing us with beautiful kitchenware and an exceptional array of versatile appliances. And we offer special thanks to Mary Rodgers.

We also thank a number of other companies that provided props for use on the set and in the book, including Mikasa, Villeroy & Boch, Present Tense, Emile Henry, Rosle, and Mango Imports.

Finally, a big thank you to our talented and hardworking production staff whose professionalism, dedication, and concern for quality is unmatchable: Scott Alpen, Brett Bailey, Todd Gardner, Nathanial Higgs, Tom Keegan, Barbara King, Kevin Parker, Deanna Sison, Mike Tillotson, Michael Varga, Gordon Winiemko, and Stan Zoerner.

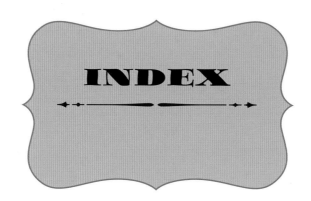

INDEX

A

anchovy
  dip, 31
  pesto, 96–97
appetizers
  aluminum foil potatoes with sexy
    sauces, 31
  caponata bruschetta, 24
  cedar-planked Brie with roasted
    garlic and peppers, 17
  grilled chilled Gulf shrimp with
    cucumbers, tomatoes, and
    peanut oil dressing, 11
  margarita wings, 32
  shrimp parfait with Lucifer cock-
    tail sauce, 27–28
apple(s)
  ginger pork chops, 77
  grilled pork loin medallions with
    turnips, caramelized onion grits,
    and, 53–54
  rings, grilled, 77
asparagus and catfish fillet, grilled,
  with potatoes, carrots, and turnips,
  102
avocado(s)
  guacamole, 27
  and shrimp butter sauce, 114
  sweet corn relish, 90

B

bacon-wrapped trout with rosemary,
  98
bagna, grilled tuna and vegetable,
  104

banana leaf–wrapped grouper with jerk
  butter and honey lemon sauce, 113
bean(s)
  black and green, tomatoes, and
    anchovy pesto, grilled mackerel
    with, 96–97
  black-eyed peas, grilled sea scallops
    with cabbage, tomatoes, slab
    bacon, and, 91
  garbanzo, grilled bison fillet with
    arugula, spicy peanut sauce,
    and, 60–61
  pulled pork sundaes, 80–81
  salad, garbanzo, 60
  spicy black, 93–94
beef
  better butter burger, 73
  bodacious T-bone steaks with sexy
    barbecue sauce, 68
  decadent steak Oscar, 72
  grilled Angus steak with assorted
    grilled peppers, grilled garlic,
    and Gorgonzola, 70
  grilled Szechuan-style skirt steak
    with white mushrooms, spinach,
    and black pepper dressing, 58
  grill wok flank steak fajitas, 75
  tagliate with arugula and grilled
    vegetables, 67
  tenderloin, jumbo shrimp wrapped
    in, 110
beet salad, red, 117

bison fillet, grilled, with arugula,
  garbanzo beans, and spicy
  peanut sauce, 60–61
bone dust barbecue spice, 29
bread. See also sandwich
  caponata bruschetta, 24
  corn, 77
broccoli, grilled pork tenderloin with
  shrimp, country ham, toasted
  peanut butter, and, 59
bruschetta, caponata, 24
burger
  better butter, 73
  garnish list, 74

C

cabbage
  coleslaw, 80–81
  grilled lamb loin with onions,
    potatoes, herbs, and, 55
  grilled sea scallops with black-eyed
    peas, tomatoes, slab bacon, and, 91
caponata bruschetta, 24
cauliflower, celery, red onion, and
  quinoa salad, 39–40
cheese
  Brie, cedar-planked, with roasted
    garlic and peppers, 17
  buffalo mozzarella, grilled veal
    chops with mushroom fricassee
    and, 78
  Camembert, grape leaf–wrapped,
    with bacon and roasted onion
    topping, 26
  Cheddar dip, spicy, 32

goat, and portobello mushroom sandwich, 21

Gorgonzola, grilled Angus steak with assorted grilled peppers, grilled garlic, and, 70

chicken

devil's brewed roast, with white trash BBQ sauce and grilled vegetable salad, 45

grilled, and vegetable fried rice, 46

grilled boneless breast of, with grapes, parsnips, and toasted almond basmati rice, 37

grilled marinated, with cauliflower, celery, red onion, and quinoa salad, 39–40

margarita wings, 32

coconut pears, grilled saddle of lamb with, 65

coleslaw, 80–81

corn

bread, 77

and chipotle stuffing, thick-cut bone-in Southwest pork chop with, 83

relish, avocado sweet, 90

vinaigrette, roasted, 22

crab(s)

cedar-planked salmon pinwheels, 116

crust, roasted red pepper, bacon, and, cedar-planked sea bass with, 118

decadent steak Oscar, 72

grilled soft-shell, grilled tomato and fennel soup with, 15–16

-meat, sautéed backfin, and grilled mahi mahi with zucchini, spinach, and cream, 89

salad, 27

cucumber(s)

grilled chilled Gulf shrimp with tomatoes, peanut oil dressing, and, 11

horseradish salad, 114–15

D

Desaulniers, Marcel, recipes by

grilled bison fillet with arugula, garbanzo beans, and spicy peanut sauce, 60–61

grilled boneless breast of chicken with grapes, parsnips, and toasted almond basmati rice, 37

grilled catfish fillet and asparagus with potatoes, carrots, and turnips, 102

grilled chilled Gulf shrimp with cucumbers, tomatoes, and peanut oil dressing, 11

grilled lamb loin with onions, potatoes, cabbage, and herbs, 55

grilled mackerel with black and green beans, tomatoes, and anchovy pesto, 96–97

grilled mahi mahi and sautéed backfin crabmeat with zucchini, spinach, and cream, 89

grilled marinated chicken with cauliflower, celery, red onion, and quinoa salad and herbed yogurt dressing, 39–40

grilled Mediterranean garden sandwich, 18

grilled monkfish with a pan roast of oysters, wild mushrooms, spinach, and leeks, 100–101

grilled pork loin medallions with apples, turnips, and caramelized onion grits, 53–54

grilled pork tenderloin with shrimp, broccoli, country ham, and toasted peanut butter, 59

grilled rainbow trout with a warm salad of grilled sweet potatoes, grapes, Belgian endive, and pumpkin seeds, 106–7

grilled salmon with chilled pink grapefruit, spicy black beans, and rice, 93–94

grilled sausage, portobello mushrooms, and vegetables with marinated French lentils, 63–64

grilled sea scallops with black-eyed peas, cabbage, tomatoes, and slab bacon, 91

grilled Szechuan-style skirt steak with white mushrooms, spinach, and black pepper dressing, 58

grilled tomato and fennel soup with grilled soft-shell crabs, 15–16

grilled veal chop with root vegetables and rosemary cream, 56

potato, leek, and watercress soup with grilled smoked duck, 13–14

dip

anchovy, 31

guacamole, 27

herbal, 31

spicy Cheddar cheese, 32

dipping sauce à la Russe, 31

direct heat cooking method, 7

doneness, cooking to correct, 6–7

duck, grilled smoked, with potato, leek, and watercress soup, 13–14

E

eggplant

caponata bruschetta, 24

stacks with roasted corn vinaigrette, 22

F

fajitas, grill wok flank steak, 75

fennel and tomato soup, grilled, with grilled soft-shell crabs, 15–16

fish. *See also* salmon; sea bass; trout
catfish fillet and asparagus, grilled, with potatoes, carrots, and turnips, 102
grouper, banana leaf–wrapped, with jerk butter and honey lemon sauce, 113
halibut, grilled, with cucumber horseradish salad and shrimp and avocado butter sauce, 114–15
mackerel, grilled, with black and green beans, tomatoes, and anchovy pesto, 96–97
mahi mahi, grilled, and sautéed backfin crabmeat with zucchini, spinach, and cream, 89
monkfish, grilled, with a pan roast of oysters, wild mushrooms, spinach, and leeks, 100–101
tuna and vegetable bagna, grilled, 104
fries, hand-cut, 41
fruit compote, curried, 84–85

G
garlic
grilled, 70
roasted, 17
grapefruit, chilled pink, grilled salmon with spicy black beans, rice, and, 93–94
grape leaf–wrapped Camembert with bacon and roasted onion topping, 26
grits, caramelized onion, 53–54
guacamole, 27

H
ham, country, grilled pork tenderloin and shrimp, broccoli, toasted peanut butter, and, 59
hash, potato, 43–44

I
indirect heat cooking method, 7

L
lamb
grilled saddle of, with coconut pears, 65
loin, grilled, with onions, potatoes, cabbage, and herbs, 55
lavender butter, 95
leek(s)
grilled monkfish with a pan roast of oysters, wild mushrooms, spinach, and, 100–101
soup, potato, watercress, and, with grilled smoked duck, 13–14
lentils, marinated French, with grilled sausage, portobello mushrooms, and vegetables, 63–64

M
mangos, grilled, with grilled salmon and lavender butter, 95
mushroom(s)
fricassee, grilled veal chops with buffalo mozzarella and, 78
portobello, and goat cheese sandwich, 21
portobello, sausage, and vegetables, grilled, with marinated French lentils, 63–64
white, grilled Szechuan-style skirt steak with spinach, black pepper dressing, and, 58
wild, grilled monkfish with a pan roast of oysters, spinach, leeks, and, 100–101

O
oysters, grilled monkfish with a pan roast of wild mushrooms, spinach, leeks, and, 100–101

P
peanut sauce, spicy, 60–61
pears, coconut, grilled saddle of lamb with, 65
pepper dressing, black, 58

pepper(s)
assorted grilled, 70
cedar-planked Brie with roasted garlic and, 17
chipotle, and corn stuffing, thick-cut bone-in Southwest pork chop with, 83
rice, bell, 93–94
pork
baby back ribs, stuffed, with curried fruit compote, 84–85
chop, thick-cut bone-in Southwest, with chipotle and corn stuffing, 83
chops, apple ginger, with grilled apple rings and corn bread, 77
loin medallions, grilled, with apples, turnips, and caramelized onion grits, 53–54
sausage, portobello mushrooms, and vegetables, grilled, with marinated French lentils, 63–64
steak, grilled, with warm potato salad, 69
sundaes, pulled, 80–81
tenderloin, grilled, with shrimp, broccoli, country ham, and toasted peanut butter, 59
potato(es)
aluminum foil, with sexy sauces, 31
grilled catfish fillet and asparagus with carrots, turnips, and, 102
grilled lamb loin with onions, cabbage, herbs, and, 55
hand-cut fries, 41
hash, 43–44
salad, warm, 69
smashed, Debbie-style, 98
soup, leek, watercress, and, with grilled smoked duck, 13–14
trout with fennel, dill, and, 105
prosciutto-wrapped salmon and scallops, 117

Q

quinoa salad, cauliflower, celery, red onion, and, 39–40

R

Reader, Ted, recipes by

banana leaf–wrapped grouper with jerk butter and honey lemon sauce, 113

better butter burger, 73

bone dust barbecue spice, 29

cedar-planked Brie with roasted garlic and peppers, 17

cedar-planked salmon pinwheels, 116

cedar-planked sea bass with roasted red pepper, crab, and bacon crust, 118

decadent steak Oscar, 72

devil's brewed roast chicken with white trash BBQ sauce and grilled vegetable salad, 45

grape leaf–wrapped Camembert with bacon and roasted onion topping, 26

grilled chicken and vegetable fried rice, 46

grilled halibut with cucumber horseradish salad and shrimp and avocado butter sauce, 114–15

grilled Thanksgiving BBQ turkey casserole, 48

grilled tuna and vegetable bagna, 104

grilled veal chops with mushroom fricassee and buffalo mozzarella, 78

grill wok flank steak fajitas, 75

margarita wings, 32

prosciutto-wrapped salmon and scallops with maple chili glaze and red beet salad, 117

pulled pork sundaes, 80–81

shrimp parfait with Lucifer cocktail sauce, 27–28

stuffed pork baby back ribs with curried fruit compote, 84–85

Texas surf and turf: jumbo shrimp wrapped in beef tenderloin, 110

thick-cut bone-in Southwest pork chop with chipotle and corn stuffing, 83

rice

bell pepper, 93–94

grilled chicken and vegetable fried, 46

toasted almond basmati, 37

S

salad

cauliflower, celery, red onion, and quinoa, 39–40

coleslaw, 80–81

crab, 27

cucumber horseradish, 114–15

garbanzo bean, 60

grilled vegetable, 45

red beet, 117

warm, of grilled sweet potatoes, grapes, Belgian endive, and pumpkin seeds, 106–7

warm potato, 69

salmon

grilled, with chilled pink grapefruit, spicy black beans, and rice, 93–94

grilled, with lavender butter and grilled mangos, 95

pinwheels, cedar-planked, 116

and scallops, prosciutto-wrapped, with maple chili glaze and red beet salad, 117

sandwich

grilled Mediterranean garden, 18

grilled tuna and vegetable bagna, 104

portobello mushroom and goat cheese, 21

sauce

barbecue, 43

dipping, à la russe, 31

Lucifer cocktail, 27

margarita wing, 32

sexy barbecue, 68

shrimp and avocado butter, 114

spicy peanut, 60–61

white trash BBQ, 45

sausage, portobello mushrooms, and vegetables, grilled, with marinated French lentils, 63–64

scallops and salmon, prosciutto-wrapped, 117

sea bass

cedar-planked, with roasted red pepper, crab, and bacon crust, 118

grilled, in aluminum foil, 108

poached, and vegetables in green peppercorn cream, 109

shrimp

and avocado butter sauce, 114

grilled, with avocado sweet corn relish, 90

grilled chilled Gulf, with cucumbers, tomatoes, and peanut oil dressing, 11

grilled pork tenderloin, broccoli, country ham, toasted peanut butter, and, 59

jumbo, wrapped in beef tenderloin, 110

parfait with Lucifer cocktail sauce, 27–28

Sonnenschmidt, Fritz, recipes by

aluminum foil potatoes with sexy sauces, 31

apple ginger pork chops with grilled apple rings and corn bread, 77

bacon-wrapped trout with rosemary and warm smashed potatoes Debbie-style, 98

bodacious T-bone steaks with sexy barbecue sauce, 68

caponata bruschetta, 24

eggplant stacks with roasted corn vinaigrette, 22

grilled Angus steak with assorted grilled peppers, grilled garlic, and Gorgonzola, 70

grilled pork steak with warm potato salad, 69

grilled saddle of lamb with coconut pears, 65

grilled salmon with lavender butter and grilled mangos, 95

grilled sea bass in aluminum foil, 108

grilled shrimp with avocado sweet corn relish, 90

grilled turkey meat loaf with hand-cut fries, 41

poached sea bass and vegetables in green peppercorn cream, 109

portobello mushroom and goat cheese sandwich, 21

tagliate with arugula and grilled vegetables, 67

trout with fennel, dill, and potatoes, 105

turkey drumsticks slathered with barbecue sauce and potato hash, 43–44

soup
  grilled tomato and fennel, with grilled soft-shell crabs, 15–16
  potato, leek, and watercress, with grilled smoked duck, 13–14

spice, bone dust barbecue, 29

sweet potatoes, grapes, Belgian endive, and pumpkin seeds, warm salad of grilled, 106–7

T

tagliate with arugula and grilled vegetables, 67

Texas surf and turf: jumbo shrimp wrapped in beef tenderloin, 110

tomato(es)
  grilled, and fennel soup with grilled soft-shell crabs, 15–16
  grilled chilled Gulf shrimp with cucumbers, peanut oil dressing, and, 11
  grilled mackerel with black and green beans, anchovy pesto, and, 96–97
  grilled Mediterranean garden sandwich, 18
  grilled sea scallops with black-eyed peas, cabbage, slab bacon, and, 91

trout
  bacon-wrapped, with rosemary and warm smashed potatoes Debbie-style, 98
  with fennel, dill, and potatoes, 105
  grilled rainbow, with a warm salad of grilled sweet potatoes, grapes, Belgian endive, and pumpkin seeds, 106–7

tuna and vegetable bagna, grilled, 104

turkey
  casserole, grilled Thanksgiving BBQ, 48
  drumsticks slathered with barbecue sauce and potato hash, 43–44
  meat loaf, grilled, with hand-cut fries, 41

V

veal
  chop, grilled, with root vegetables and rosemary cream, 56
  chops, grilled, with mushroom fricassee and buffalo mozzarella, 78

vegetable(s). *See also individual vegetables*
  grilled, tagliate with arugula and, 67
  and grilled chicken fried rice, 46
  grilled sausage, portobello mushrooms, and, with marinated French lentils, 63–64
  root, grilled veal chop with rosemary cream and, 56
  salad, grilled, 45
  and sea bass, poached, in green peppercorn cream, 109
  and tuna bagna, grilled, 104

W

watercress, potato, and leek soup with grilled smoked duck, 13–14

wok flank steak fajitas, grill, 75

Z

zucchini, grilled mahi mahi and sautéed backfin crabmeat with spinach, cream, and, 89

NOTES

NOTES